Alcohol
Use Among
Adolescents

Developmental Clinical Psychology and Psychiatry Series

Series Editor: Alan E. Kazdin, Yale University

Recent volumes in this series . . .

Alcohol Use Among Adolescents

Michael Windle

Volume 42
Developmental Clinical Psychology and Psychiatry

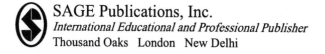 SAGE Publications, Inc.
International Educational and Professional Publisher
Thousand Oaks   London   New Delhi

For information:

SAGE Publications, Inc.
2455 Teller Road
Thousand Oaks, California 91320
E-mail: order@sagepub.com

SAGE Publications Ltd.
6 Bonhill Street
London EC2A 4PU
United Kingdom

SAGE Publications India Pvt. Ltd.
M-32 Market
Greater Kailash I
New Delhi 110 048 India

Printed in the United States of America

Library of Congress Cataloging-in-Publication Data

Windle, Michael T.
    Alcohol use among adolescents / by Michael Windle.
    p. cm. — (Developmental clinical psychology and psychiatry
series; v. 42)
    Includes bibliographical references and index.
    ISBN 0-7619-0919-2 (cloth: acid-free paper)
    ISBN 0-7619-0920-6 (pbk.: acid-free paper)
    2. Teenagers—Alcohol use. 2. Alcoholism—Prevention. I. Title.
II. Series; Developmental clinical psychology and psychiatry; v. 42.
    RJ506.A4 W557   1999
    616.86′1′00835—dc21   99-6110

99 00 01 02 03 04 05 10 9 8 7 6 5 4 3 2 1

Acquiring Editor:	Jim Nageotte
Editorial Assistant:	Heidi Van Middlesworth
Production Editor:	Wendy Westgate
Editorial Assistant:	Patricia Zeman
Designer/Typesetter:	Janelle LeMaster
Cover Designer:	Candice Harman

CONTENTS

SERIES EDITOR'S INTRODUCTION

Interest in child development and adjustment is by no means new. Yet only recently has the study of children benefited from advances in both clinical and scientific research. Advances in the social and biological sciences, the emergence of disciplines and subdisciplines that focus exclusively on childhood and adolescence, and greater appreciation of the impact of such influences as the family, peers, and school have helped accelerate research on developmental psychopathology. Apart from interest in the study of child development and adjustment for its own sake, the need to address clinical problems of adulthood naturally draws one to investigate precursors in childhood and adolescence.

Within a relatively brief period, the study of psychopathology among children and adolescents has grown considerably. Several different professional journals, annual book series, and handbooks devoted entirely to the study of children and adolescents and their adjustment document the proliferation of work in the field. Nevertheless, there is a paucity of resource material that presents information in an authoritative, systematic, and disseminable fashion. There is a need within the field to convey the latest developments and to represent different disciplines, approaches, and conceptual views to the topics of childhood and adolescent adjustment and maladjustment.

The Sage Series **Developmental Clinical Psychology and Psychiatry** is designed to serve several needs of the field. The Series encompasses individual monographs prepared by experts in the fields of clinical child psychology, child psychiatry, child development, and related disciplines. The primary focus is on developmental psychopathology, which here broadly refers to the diagnosis, assessment, treatment, and prevention of problems that arise in the period from infancy through adolescence. A working assumption of the Series is that understanding, identifying, and treating problems of youth must draw on multiple disciplines and diverse views within a given discipline.

The task for individual contributors is to present the latest theory and research on various topics, including specific types of dysfunction, diagnostic and treatment approaches, and special problem areas that affect adjustment. Core topics within clinical work are addressed by the Series. Authors are asked to bridge potential theory, research, and clinical practice and to outline the current status and future directions. The goals of the Series and the tasks presented to individual contributors are demanding. We have been extremely fortunate in recruiting leaders in the fields who have been able to translate their recognized scholarship and expertise into highly readable works on contemporary topics.

In this book, Dr. Michael Windle examines alcohol use among adolescents. This book carefully documents the latest research on the scope of the problem, assessment, diagnosis, screening youth for alcohol use, risk and protective factors, treatment, prevention, and social-policy-based intervention programs. Among the many topics that are covered are the relation of alcohol use to substance abuse more generally; biological, psychological, and contextual influences on adolescent drinking; and ethnic, cultural, and gender-based variations in patterns of alcohol use over the course of development. There is a remarkable balance in the coverage of conceptual models of the problem, empirical research, and methodological challenges in evaluating alcohol use over the course of development. The book is forward looking in suggesting promising leads for understanding etiology and effective interventions and in pointing to several lines of research that are priorities for the upcoming years. Dr. Windle's own research on the interrelation of alcohol use to other domains of functioning in adolescents, alcohol use at different points in development, and key developmental themes (e.g., peer relations, cognitive functioning, and sex differences) make this book broad in scope and developmentally informed. The book conveys the significance of adolescent alcohol use as a social and clinical problem and also points to promising leads for its amelioration.

—*ALAN E. KAZDIN, Ph.D.*

PREFACE

Adolescent alcohol use is pervasive in the United States, with the vast majority of adolescents having consumed alcohol by their senior year of high school. However, public knowledge that most adolescents use alcohol by their senior year of high school provides the health care community and social policymakers with little guidance as to the prevalence of different patterns of drinking behavior (e.g., light versus heavy drinking), the presumed underlying causes of drinking, or the optimal ways to intervene to reduce or eliminate alcohol use among youth. The study of adolescent alcohol use is an interdisciplinary endeavor, with disciplinary contributions from epidemiologists, biologists, clinical and developmental psychologists, psychiatrists, pediatricians, economists, counselors, nurses, and educators. Many of these professionals are concerned with common issues about adolescent alcohol use but due to time constraints and the proliferation of profession-specific journals, they may not be cognizant of relevant research in cognate professions. Likewise, researchers in other specialty areas, graduate students, and health care professionals often seek resources that provide a relatively rapid overview of key issues in a field such as adolescent alcohol use.

This book attempts to provide representative coverage to a broad and rapidly expanding literature on adolescent alcohol use. Chapter 1 provides an introduction to the scope of issues related to adolescent alcohol use, including data on the prevalence of various alcohol use indicators, such as frequency of use and binge drinking. In Chapter 2, a review is provided of approaches to the measurement of alcohol-related behaviors among adolescents, drawing on strategies used in both social survey and clinical diagnostic traditions. Chapter 3 reviews literature that has identified a large number of risk and protective factors for adolescent alcohol use. In Chapter 4, literature is reviewed pertinent to a range of psychosocial, community, and social policy interventions that have attempted to reduce adolescent alcohol use and related problems. Findings from the treatment literature are also included in this chapter. Chapter 5 focuses on some major conceptual and methodological issues that the field of adolescent alcohol use must confront to advance the field toward more optimal solutions for the drinking behaviors of youth. I am indebted to the National Institute on Alcoholism and Alcohol Abuse for their ongoing support of my research on adolescent alcohol use. The support of a Method-to-Extend Research in Time Award (R37AA07861) has significantly affected my career development in adolescent alcohol use and enabled me to broaden my horizons for subsequent research in the field. I am also indebted to my colleagues at the Research Institute on Addictions in Buffalo, New York, where I conducted research for 11 years prior to assuming my current position. I am particularly grateful to Dr. Howard Blane who assisted me early in my career development in the study of adolescent alcohol use. I am also grateful to Peggy Nicholson, my Administrative Assistant, for her technical assistance in preparing this monograph. She was patient and helpful through my many revisions of this book. Last, but certainly not least, I am quite grateful to my wife, Rebecca Windle, who served as a sounding board and editor for much of the material presented in this book. She willingly assisted in this endeavor and was especially pleased (I daresay ecstatic) when it was sent off to the publishers.

1

SCOPE OF
ADOLESCENT ALCOHOL USE
An Introduction

Adolescent alcohol use is statistically normative behavior in the United States. By their senior year of high school, the vast majority of adolescents have drunk alcohol at some point in their lifetime, with a substantial subset of adolescents drinking at high levels and experiencing a range of serious alcohol-related problems (e.g., Johnston, O'Malley, & Bachman, 1991, 1996; White & Labouvie, 1989). The occurrence of a heavy drinking episode (i.e., having five or more drinks on a single occasion) was reported by about 25% of 10th graders and 33% of 12th graders (Johnston et al., 1996), and the average age of alcohol use initiation (or first drink) has decreased from 17.8 years in 1987 to 15.9 years in 1996 (Office of National Drug Control Policy, 1997). Alcohol use among teens has been associated with the three most common forms of adolescent mortality, specifically accidental deaths (e.g., fatal automobile or boat crashes), homicides, and suicides. On average, eight adolescents a day die in alcohol-related fatal automobile crashes in the United States, and 9 out of 10 teenage automobile accidents involve the use of alcohol (Office of National Drug Control Policy [ONDCP], 1997). With a national school sample, Windle, Miller-Tutzauer, and Domenico (1992) reported that suicide attempts among heavy-drinking adolescents were three to four times greater than for abstainers.

In addition to significant associations with the three leading causes of adolescent mortality, alcohol use among adolescents is significantly associated with a range of other health-compromising behaviors. Higher levels of alcohol use are associated with more frequent, often unprotected, sexual activity among adolescents, which poses increased risk for teen pregnancy and sexually transmitted diseases, including potentially life-threatening dis-

1

eases such as human immunodeficiency virus. An earlier onset of alcohol use and higher levels of use among adolescents has been associated with poorer academic functioning (e.g., lower grade point average, more unexcused absences) and higher rates of school dropout. Alcohol use has also commonly been described as a "gateway" substance, with the use of alcohol preceding the use of marijuana and marijuana use preceding the use of other harder drugs, such as cocaine, heroin, hallucinogens, and so forth (e.g., Kandel, 1985).

In discussing these relatively strong and consistent associations between alcohol use and indicators of mortality and behavioral health problems among adolescents, it is important to note that definitive causal relations have yet to be firmly established in most instances and that in other instances, alcohol is not necessarily posited as a causal variable. For example, the use of alcohol typically occurs prior to the onset of marijuana, which, in turn, typically occurs prior to the onset of hard drug use. The theoretical argument for preventive intervention efforts with alcohol as the gateway substance is not that alcohol *causes* marijuana use but rather that most individuals who use hard drugs preceded their use of these substances with marijuana and preceded the use of marijuana with alcohol. Most adolescents who use alcohol do not become marijuana and hard drug addicts. The gateway notion as applied to prevention suggests that a delay in the onset of alcohol use may decrease the probability of progressing to more serious levels of substance use because, across time, adolescents become older and more mature and presumably better able to make informed, healthy lifestyle choices. Thus, although explanatory mechanisms that account for the causal relations between alcohol-health outcome relations are not always well substantiated or even necessarily postulated, alcohol use and alcohol-influenced intervening processes (e.g., behavioral disinhibition, motor response slowing, perceptual difficulties) are associated with a wide range of health-related problems among adolescents. Because of the pervasiveness of associations between alcohol use and health-compromising behaviors, preventive intervention approaches for adolescent alcohol use have become a critical focus of much current scientific research.

BRIEF HISTORY OF ALCOHOL USE

Alcohol has been ingested by humankind since the earliest recorded writings and art works. The use of beer was documented in Babylon in 4000 B.C., the use of wine in Egypt in 3000 B.C., and the use of hard liquors in China in 800 B.C. Throughout history, alcohol has been a commonly consumed beverage for multiple purposes, including those associated with celebrations (e.g., weddings, award ceremonies, funerals), religious ceremonies, and social and recreational events. Perhaps because of its common consumption, moral and legal prohibitions against alcohol use have not been successful in eliminating the imbibing of spirits. For example, the temperance movement for legal prohibition of alcohol during the early part of the 20th century did not meet with success, and Prohibition was repealed in 1933.

From colonial times to the 18th century in the United States, alcohol use was quite common among men and women, as local taverns were major settings for relaxation, town meetings, and political discussions (e.g., Rorabaugh, 1979). Drinking decreased substantially in the 19th century as per capita alcohol consumption deceased between 1830 and 1850 from a high of five gallons per person a year to 2.5 gallons a year (Fingarette, 1989). This change has been attributed to social, economic, and intellectual changes in the 19th century, including advances in medical science in general and disease processes in particular.

In the United States, the legal use of alcohol by individuals currently identified within the adolescent age range (ages 13-20 years old) was quite common from colonial times until the late 1800s and early 1900s (Mosher, 1980). Oftentimes, many of these adolescents worked in the fields or mines with adults and were therefore afforded similar privileges with regard to access to alcohol. Even younger children and adolescents were permitted to consume alcoholic beverages if their parents approved of such use. Mosher also reported that youthful drinking per se was not a primary target of the temperance movement. However, the greater involvement by the state during the early to mid-1900s on a range of social issues (e.g., compulsory education) led to more specific age-related drinking laws, with associated sanctions for violations either by the adolescent or the merchant selling to adolescents.

Despite these enacted laws related to youthful drinking, underage drinking increased steadily from 1930 to 1960 (Mosher, 1980). During the past 30 to 35 years, research studies regarding alcohol use by adolescents (and by adults) have increased substantially, with annual surveys to monitor usage patterns. Federal and private research funds have also been allocated to study causes and consequences of adolescent alcohol use, as well as the development and application of preventive intervention programs to ameliorate or eliminate alcohol use by adolescents.

ALCOHOL USE, SUBSTANCE USE, AND CONDUCT PROBLEMS

The focus of this volume is on adolescent alcohol use rather than all substances of use (e.g., nicotine, cocaine, heroin, amphetamines). There are some important distinctions that differentiate substance use practices by adolescents, as well as the public response to such use. Across all 50 states in the United States, the legal drinking age is 21 years; furthermore, although there are "dry" counties in many states (where alcoholic beverages are not sold), alcohol is a legal substance for adult purchase and consumption. Alcohol advertising (especially beer advertising) is widely practiced and is often associated with passive leisure activities (e.g., musical concerts, professional sporting events) attended by millions of children, adolescents, and adults. Although alcohol use by adolescents is generally not condoned by adults, many parents view infrequent, low levels of use by older adolescents as relatively innocuous. In contrast, hard drugs, such as cocaine or heroin, are illegal substances for both adolescents and adults, public advertising (e.g., television ads) is not legal, and adults are much less tolerant (and more punitive) about any level of adolescent use of these substances.

Cigarette (nicotine) use among adolescents presents yet a third distinct situation. Cigarettes are legal substances about which there is substantial advertising (much of it geared toward youth) and fairly widespread use among adolescents and adults. Three thousand children or adolescents initiate regular cigarette smoking daily (ONDCP, 1997). However, contrary to the potential immediate detrimental effects of alcohol on adolescent behavior (e.g., drinking and driving accidents, violence, attempted or completed suicides), the effect of nicotine is more subtle (e.g., does not impair motor performance) and its detrimental effects are more long-term (e.g., cancer or cardiovascular disease after many years of heavy smoking). Hence, although alcohol, cigarette, and drug use are often significantly correlated, there are a number of important distinctions in terms of legal and social-cultural dimensions, as well as underlying biochemistry and psychopharmacology.

At times, alcohol use has been conceptualized as a symptom, or characteristic, of delinquency, conduct problems, or antisocial behaviors. As a symptom of a broader constellation of early-onset (childhood) conduct problems, this may be beneficial for some research purposes. However, to view all alcohol use exclusively as a symptom of conduct problems or antisocial behaviors is not warranted on the basis of the extant literature, as will be illustrated in this volume. There are many aspects of alcohol-related behaviors (age of onset, frequency and quantity of use, heavy drinking episodes, adverse social consequences) that preclude the reduction of childhood or adolescent alcohol use to a single symptom. Furthermore, there are many adolescents who use alcohol who do not engage in high levels of conduct problems; therefore, there is no intrinsic relationship between alcohol use and conduct problems to suggest that they somehow reflect a common, underlying dimension or genotype. This is not to suggest that conduct problems may not be an important precursor to alcohol abuse for some adolescents or that there may not be some common underlying mechanisms (e.g., high behavioral disinhibition), but rather it is to suggest that alcohol use is not optimally viewed solely as a symptom of conduct problems.

BIOLOGICAL ASPECTS OF ALCOHOL

There are different kinds of alcohol, but the kind referenced in this book is ethyl alcohol or ethanol. This alcohol is a product of the fermentation of sugars, starches, or other carbohydrates. Fermentation involves the development of yeast enzymes that convert sugar to ethyl alcohol. The fermentation of grapes and other fruits yields wine; the fermentation of grain or honey yields beer; and the fermentation and distillation of grapes, grains, molasses, or other sugars and starches yields liquors (Kumar & O'Brien, 1994). Distillation concentrates the alcohol, and hence the alcohol concentration in liquors is typically substantially higher than in beer or wine. Although there is variation in the amount of alcohol (or alcoholic content) within each of the beer, wine, and liquor categories, in general, in the United States, beer consists of approximately 5% alcohol, wine consists of about 13% to 14% alcohol, and liquor consists of 40% to 45% alcohol (though some liquors are 80% alcohol).

Pharmacologically, alcohol is a sedative with regard to its influence on the central nervous system (CNS). The sedating effects of alcohol initially reduce CNS inhibitory processes and as such, after a drink or two, people subjectively report feeling more relaxed, less constrained socially, and more talkative; such feeling states as more talkativeness and greater sociability often contribute to the misconception that alcohol is a stimulant.

Research efforts to understand the influence of alcohol use on a variety of behaviors (e.g., psychomotor performance, aggression, mood fluctuations) have focused on the *biphasic effects* of alcohol ingestion. Subsequent to consuming alcohol, the blood alcohol concentration (BAC) level follows a biphasic trajectory, in that there is an initial increase in the BAC level followed by a decrease that is associated with alcohol absorption and elimination. The initial increasing phase is referred to as the *ascending limb* of the BAC curve, and it is associated with stimulation, arousal, activation, and euphoria. The decreasing phase of the BAC curve is referred to as the *descending limb,* and it is associated with sedation, dysphoria, and negative mood states. A large number of studies have supported reliable differences in mood, arousal, behavior (e.g., aggression), and neuropsychological functioning contingent on the phase (ascending or descending limb) of the BAC curve (e.g., Giancola & Zeichner, 1997; Martin, Earlywine, Musty, Perrine, & Swift, 1993). Furthermore, it has been suggested that heavier drinking is influenced by efforts to retain the euphoric states associated with the ascending limb and thereby avoiding the dysphoric states associated with the descending limb.

Although the effects of alcohol on the brain are not yet fully known, recent research on animal models (e.g., Koob & Bloom, 1988) and a limited number of studies on humans (e.g., Ingvar et al., 1998) supports the notion that alcohol activates reward (or pleasure) centers in the brain. This activation of the reward center and the associated positive reinforcement has provided a parsimonious theory both for the persistence of alcohol consumption to the level of an alcohol disorder and for targeted pharmacologic agents (e.g., selective serotonin reuptake inhibitors) to block the rewarding aspects of alcohol consumption.

Other biologically influenced processes resulting from the prolonged, heavy use of alcohol are *tolerance* and *withdrawal.* Alcohol tolerance refers to a need for significant increases in the consumption of alcohol to achieve the same level of intoxication or desired state. Thus, 4 to 5 drinks may produce a desired level of intoxication among individuals when they initiate drinking, but across time, with continued drinking, 9 to 10 drinks may be required to attain the same desired level of intoxication. (There are a variety of cellular adaptations and molecular mechanisms that are associated with tolerance, but coverage of this is beyond the scope of this book.) Alcohol withdrawal refers to a range of physical and psychological responses that accompany efforts to reduce or stop the consumption of alcohol, such as autonomic hyperactivity or nausea and anxiety states.

The importance of this succinct description of some of the biological aspects of alcohol is to highlight a few features that are relevant for understanding adolescent alcohol use. Alcohol use, unlike psychiatric disorders, requires adolescents to actively choose to engage in beverage consumption. This is not to suggest that there are not strong biological and environmental factors operating to influence drinking behaviors but only suggests that the (initial) voluntary nature of this activity differs, say, from the onset of a depressive disorder. In addition to social rewards that may be associated with the consumption of alcohol among adolescents (e.g., as a peer-based shared activity, as a facilitator of social activities at parties), there is a biological basis that links alcohol consumption with the pleasure center in the brain; hence, alcohol consumption may be associated with positive reinforcement at both biological and psychosocial levels of analyses.

The underlying biochemistry and physiology of the human organism (e.g., cellular adaptation, neurotransmitter systems) interact with levels of alcohol consumption to contribute to altered biological system functioning as manifested in processes such as tolerance and withdrawal. As such, many adolescents (and adults) may engage in alcohol use because of the associated biological and social rewards. However, there is wide variability in biological responses to alcohol, with genetic factors contributing to quite adverse responses by some individuals and more rewarding effects in others. An understanding of the role of alcohol on biological systems and on the particular biological vulnerabilities of adolescents has yet to be systematically explored, though such knowledge will eventually be required for a comprehensive understanding of adolescent drinking behaviors.

EPIDEMIOLOGY OF ALCOHOL-RELATED BEHAVIORS AMONG ADOLESCENTS

The systematic, large-scale study of adolescent alcohol-related behaviors (e.g., alcohol use, alcohol problems, heavy or binge drinking episodes) is, historically and scientifically speaking, a relatively recent phenomenon. Among the most long-standing and well-known U.S. national studies of substance use (including alcohol use) among adolescents is the Monitoring the Future Studies (MFS) (e.g., Johnston et al., 1996), which were initiated circa 1975 to provide national surveillance data on adolescent substance use practices. The MFS has, since its inception, provided annual national surveys of adolescent substance use practices and associated attitudes about various features of substance use (e.g., perceived harmfulness, perceived availability). Over approximately the first 20 years of the MFS, the annual survey samples consisted solely of high school seniors.

In recent years, the MFS has expanded in two significant ways. First, the number of grade levels has been extended to include earlier grade levels (e.g., 8th and 10th graders); this is important because of historical trends in substance use that indicate an earlier age of onset for substance use among children (ONDCP, 1997). Second, there has been increasing interest in substance use practices in young adulthood and in the longitudinal relations between substance use practices in adolescence and their longer-term impact on functioning in young adulthood (e.g., in relation to age-normative role functioning in occupational, marital, and parental contexts) (e.g., Jessor, Donovan, & Costa, 1991; Schulenberg, Wadsworth, O'Malley, Bachman, & Johnston, 1996).

In addition to the MFS, there have been several other large-scale studies of adolescent alcohol and drug use, some of them nationally or regionally representative in scope (e.g., Barnes & Welte, 1986; Windle, 1991). The following presentation of epidemiological findings about adolescent alcohol use are based largely on the MFS (Johnston et al., 1996); other regional or local studies are cited to substantiate other significant considerations.

The data provided in Figure 1.1 indicate that the prevalence of using alcohol increases across grade levels for all three racial-ethnic groups. However, it is important to note that by eighth grade, over 50% of these children report having consumed an alcoholic beverage. Racial-ethnic group differences indicate a particularly high prevalence of lifetime alcohol use among Hispanic children. Similar to findings in previous studies (Barnes & Welte, 1986; Windle, 1991), black adolescents have the lowest rate of lifetime alcohol use. Research findings from earlier MFS cohorts (e.g., Bachman et al., 1991) and from other epidemiological studies (e.g., Barnes & Welte, 1986) have also indicated very high (if not the highest) prevalence of lifetime alcohol use among Native American children and adolescents, as well as quite low rates among Asian Americans. Parenthetically, it should be recognized that drinking practices among adolescents (and adults) may vary considerably for subgroups (e.g., for different Native American tribes, for Mexican Americans versus Puerto Ricans) within the broad racial-ethnic groups used to present these data.

In addition to lifetime use of alcohol, another useful index of trends in adolescent drinking references heavy or "binge" drinking episodes. *Binge drinking* refers to the consumption of five or more drinks in a single setting over the past 2 weeks. In contrast to lifetime alcohol use, the binge-drinking index is designed to assess potentially problematic drinking that may contribute to current problems (e.g., poorer school performance, greater risk in drinking and driving) and be prognostic of longer-term difficulties. The data presented in Figure 1.2 indicate both high rates of binge drinking and increases across grade levels. Differences are also indicated for the three racial-ethnic groups. Hispanic adolescents had substantially higher rates of binge drinking than whites or blacks among 8th graders and then small increases for 10th and 12th graders. Black adolescents had the lowest preva-

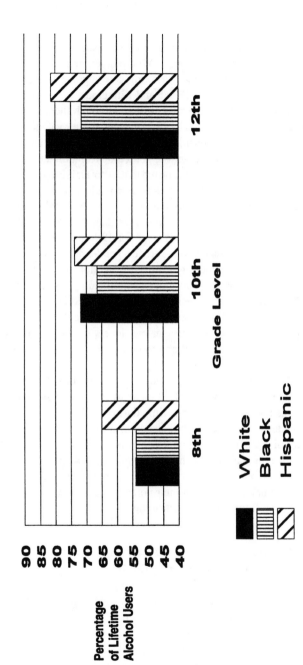

Figure 1.1. Racial-Ethnic Comparisons of Lifetime Alcohol Use by Grade Level
SOURCE: Adapted from Monitoring the Future Survey (Johnston et al., 1996).

lence of binge drinking across all three grade levels, substantially lower than their white and Hispanic counterparts. White adolescents had the greatest increases in the prevalence of binge drinking across grade levels, with 8th graders reporting a prevalence of 13.9% and 12th graders reporting a prevalence of 32.3%. Hence, these data suggest that, although there is variability across age (grade levels) and racial-ethnic groups, the prevalence of binge drinking among adolescents, considered collectively, is quite high.

Gender provides yet another potential source of variation among adolescent drinking practices. It has been proposed that historical shifts toward more gender equality in work and family roles among adults may be contributing to a convergence in drinking practices among male and female adolescents (White & Huselid, 1997). Figure 1.3 provides data collected in the MFS (Johnston et al., 1996) relevant to this issue for 12th graders. If lifetime or past year (annual) use is evaluated, there are few gender differences in alcohol use. However, for more serious indicators of alcohol use, such as binge drinking and daily alcohol use, boys have a significantly higher prevalence than girls. These findings are consistent with other studies (e.g., White & Huselid, 1997; Windle, 1996) in supporting the inference that boys are more likely than girls to engage in more serious levels of alcohol use (more frequently and at higher quantities) and to have more alcohol-related problems.

In summary, these epidemiological findings provide a broad picture of the drinking practices of adolescents. It is evident that the vast majority of adolescents consume alcohol at some time during adolescence, with a substantial number also engaging in binge-drinking episodes. The study of more extensive alcohol problems among adolescents is a relatively recent phenomena, but the current data highlight high rates of such problems among adolescents (e.g., White & Labouvie, 1989; Windle, 1996). These alcohol problems are of concern because of their potential compromising influences on both current and future health functioning.

EPIDEMIOLOGY OF ADOLESCENT ALCOHOL DISORDERS

As the preceding information demonstrates, data on adolescent alcohol use practices has increased substantially over the past 25 years or so. However, these national and regional survey studies have not included data on the number of adolescents meeting formal clinical diagnostic criteria for alcohol disorders. The available evidence, based on a few recent community studies,

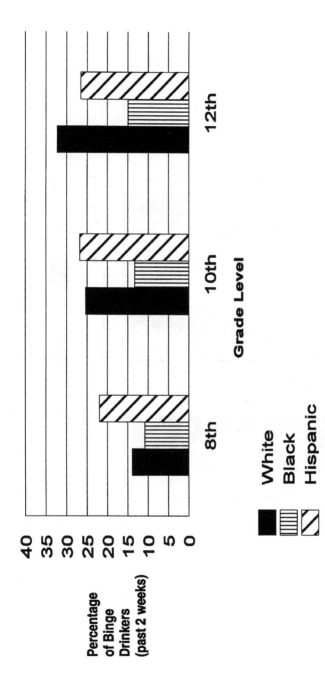

Figure 1.2. Racial-Ethnic Comparisons of Binge Drinking by Grade Level
SOURCE: Adapted from Monitoring the Future Survey (Johnston et al., 1996).

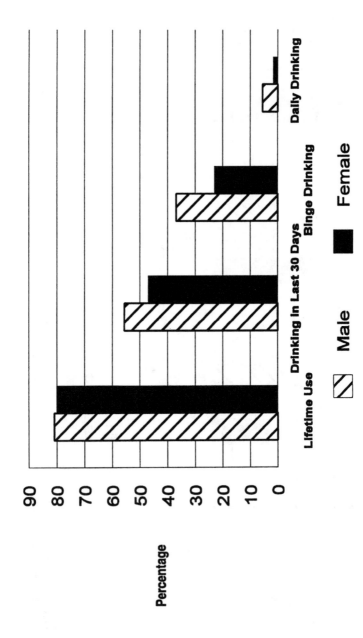

Figure 1.3. Gender Comparisons for Indicators of Alcohol Use Among 12th Graders
SOURCE: Adapted from Monitoring the Future Survey (Johnston et al., 1996.

suggests that between 3% and 32% of adolescents meet lifetime criteria for alcohol disorders (e.g., Cohen et al., 1993; Reinherz, Giaconia, Lefkowitz, Pakiz, & Frost, 1993). In the Cohen et al. (1993) study, the lower rate of 3% to 4% was reported for a subsample that included an age range of 14 to 16 years; the prevalence for the subsample in the age range of 17 to 20 years was 8.9% for girls and 20.3% for boys. Kashani et al. (1987) reported a prevalence rate of 5.3% for alcohol disorders among a community sample of adolescents aged 15 years. Reinherz et al. (1993) studied 386 older adolescents, mostly seniors in high school with an average age of 17.9 years. For these adolescents, 32.4% met the Diagnostic and Statistical Manual of Mental Disorders, 3rd Edition, Revised (DSM-III-R; American Psychiatric Association [APA], 1987) criteria for a lifetime alcohol disorder, with almost three quarters of those meeting the criteria classified as either moderately or severely dependent. Boys (37.6%) were more highly represented than girls (26.8%) with regard to the prevalence of an alcohol disorder. With a community sample of 3,021 adolescents and young adults (aged 14 to 24 years) in Munich, Germany, 25.1% of men and 7.0% of women met DSM-IV (APA, 1994) diagnostic criteria for an alcohol disorder (Holly & Wittchen, 1998). Furthermore, a cumulative plot of the incidence of alcohol disorders indicated initial incidence at age 13 to 14 years, with a rapid acceleration to a peak at 15 to 17 years, followed by a gradual decrease thereafter. Cultural differences between the United States and Germany may contribute to this somewhat earlier onset of heavier alcohol involvement by German youth. Nevertheless, it is evident that the prevalence of alcohol disorders among adolescents is sufficiently high to merit increased concern and responsiveness from those concerned with the health and welfare of our youth.

THEORIES AND MODELS OF ADOLESCENT ALCOHOL USE

Notwithstanding the relative recency with which alcohol use among adolescents has become a topic of scientific interest, there have been a number of theories and conceptual models designed to account for such drinking behavior. Although numerous ways exist to represent these various theories and models (e.g., Pagliaro & Pagliaro, 1996; Petraitis, Flay, & Miller, 1995), here I briefly summarize four types of models that make different assumptions about the primary underlying causes of adolescent alcohol and drug use. The four types of models are (a) biogenetic and dispositional models, (b) socialization models, (c) multivariate models, and (d) dynamic contextual models.

Biogenetic and Dispositional Models

Research in behavioral genetics has indicated that alcoholism is a heritable disorder (e.g., Heath, 1995; McGue, 1994). Furthermore, research has provided support for a genetically influenced alcoholism subtype characterized by a pattern of early alcohol onset and persistent childhood (and adult) conduct problems and criminal behaviors (e.g., Cloninger, Bohman, & Sigvardsson, 1981). Tarter (1988) proposed that deviations from the norm in underlying temperamental attributes, such as high activity level, may contribute to ongoing dysregulated behavioral cycles that yield different manifestations of dysfunction throughout the lifespan. Temperament attributes are highly heritable, and temperament deviations in, for example, high activity level, may contribute to conduct problems and early-onset drinking in childhood, more serious involvement in alcohol use and alcohol problems in adolescence, and alcohol and substance abuse disorders in adulthood. Tarter's model specifically attempts to identify temperamental deviations that may be predictive of the early onset, antisocial alcoholic subtype identified by Cloninger et al. (1981).

Arnett (1992) proposed that sensation seeking, a biologically influenced temperament attribute, and adolescent egocentrism, in concert with socialization influences, account for drinking and other risky behaviors among adolescents. Arnett's developmental account suggests that a propensity for reckless behavior, including alcohol use, is a common feature of adolescence and not necessarily an aberrant or deviant behavior. He garnered support for his perspective in reviewing literature that indicated that the height of sensation seeking is age 16 years, with subsequent declines that accompany aging. High sensation seeking reflects a need for varied novel stimuli and the desire to experience new sensations and events. Hence, high sensation seeking, in and of itself, is not a disposition toward substance abuse, criminality, or psychopathology. Arnett also suggested that adolescent egocentrism may foster personal fables of invulnerability, whereby adolescents believe that they are exempt from adverse consequences associated with reckless behaviors. The combination of higher sensation seeking and egocentrism among adolescents provides a developmental context for the engagement in reckless behaviors, such as alcohol use. Arnett argues, however, that the interaction between these dispositional features and multiple socialization influences (e.g., family, peers, media) contributes to the frequency, diversity, and severity of manifestations of reckless behaviors.

Sher (1991) reviewed a somewhat extensive literature on individual differences in the pharmacological effects of alcohol that may influence adolescent (and adult) alcohol use. In brief, two potential mechanisms have been proposed. The first is that there are individual differences in sensitivity to the reinforcing effects of alcohol. That is, there is individual variation in the positively reinforcing value of alcohol to reduce stress and to produce more euphoric effects on mood states. Thus, those with a pharmacologic disposition to experience more positively reinforcing effects from alcohol may be at increased risk for more frequent and heavier alcohol use and alcohol problems. Second, there has been mixed support for differential initial sensitivity to the effects of alcohol. The proposal is that some individuals are less sensitive to the consumption of alcohol and therefore drink more to achieve given desired mood states. This higher level of consumption may lead to adverse consequences. Other individuals who are more pharmacologically sensitive to alcohol may curb or stop their drinking prior to levels that are associated with more adverse consequences. Neither of these two pharmacologic mechanisms has been extensively studied with adolescents, though to the extent that they are apt characterizations of alcohol vulnerability, they certainly could pose risk for adolescent drinking.

Socialization Models

There is a broad range of models that could fit under this umbrella, so the focus will be on two exemplars. Socialization models typically rely on social learning theory as a theoretical backdrop and on learning mechanisms (e.g., imitation, role modeling) to describe the phenomena of interest. Kandel (1980) has emphasized the importance of the interpersonal domains of parents and peers in accounting for adolescent substance use. She cites data supportive of the role of imitation, in that parental attitudes and behaviors regarding substance use are significantly associated with offspring's attitudes and behaviors regarding substance use. The imitative behavior of substance use by adolescents is then followed by a socially reinforcing consolidation phase in which substance use behaviors and beliefs are internalized by adolescents. Peer selection and socialization processes may serve as a further basis of social reinforcement for substance use and for the internalization of substance-using beliefs and behaviors.

Brook, Brook, Gordon, Whiteman, and Cohen (1990) have extended the socialization model in their family interactional framework. This framework emphasizes the importance of a close attachment between parents and adolescents as central to understanding adolescent substance use. A strong parent-adolescent bond, characterized by strong identification, lack of conflict, affectional warmth, and parental involvement in adolescent concerns, serves as a protective factor against adolescent involvement in substances. Although underscoring the significance of the parent-adolescent bond, Brook et al. embed the family within a broader social-ecological context, which includes acculturative and school influences, as well as personality and behavior traits that may affect family functioning, the parent-adolescent bond, and ultimately, adolescent alcohol use. Barnes (1990) has also extensively reviewed literature supportive of the importance of the family and of parent-child (adolescent) relations in predicting adolescent alcohol use.

Multivariate Models

Jessor and colleagues (e.g., Donovan & Jessor, 1978; Jessor et al., 1991; Jessor & Jessor, 1977) provide a more extensively articulated model of adolescent alcohol use within the context of Problem Behavior Theory (PBT). According to PBT, there is a syndrome of problem behaviors displayed in adolescence that includes alcohol and drug use, sexual activity, general deviant behavior, and low commitment to conventional behaviors, such as academic performance and church attendance. The occurrence of these behaviors in adolescence is precipitated by the transition from childhood (or adolescence) to adult status. That is, the maturity of adult status is highly valued by adolescents, and hence they engage in a number of behaviors that are part of the adult repertoire.

The full conceptual model of Jessor and colleagues (e.g., Donovan & Jessor, 1978; Jessor et al., 1991; Jessor & Jessor, 1977) involves three major systems: (a) the Personality System that includes motivational (e.g., value on independence, value on academic achievement), personal belief (e.g., self-esteem), and personal control (e.g., attitudinal tolerance of deviance) structures; (b) the Perceived Environment System that includes distal (e.g., parental support and control) and proximal (e.g., friends' approval of problem behavior) structures; and (c) the Behavior System, which includes both problem behaviors and ties to conventional structures. It is proposed that these three systems interact with one another and are influenced by antecedent and background features, such as socioeconomic status (SES) and socialization influences (e.g., maternal and paternal traditional beliefs and tolerance of deviance), in predicting the expression of adolescent problem behaviors, including alcohol use and problem drinking. Therefore, this conceptualization posits that multiple personal and structural variables (e.g., perceived family and peer attitudes and beliefs) interact to predict the expression of deviance-prone activities, such as alcohol use.

Huba and Bentler (1982) also proposed a multivariate interactional model to provide a conceptual framework for investigating adolescent substance use. The model identified the four domains of biological factors (genetic influences), intrapersonal factors (cognitive, affective, and personality variables), interpersonal factors (intimate support system), and sociocultural factors (social sanctions, product availability) as necessary components to understand adolescent substance use. Furthermore, these authors argued for the need to study the interrelations and interactions among these variables across time with advanced statistical modeling techniques (e.g., structural equation modeling) to evaluate the plausibility of proposed causal relations among variables. Although the domain model of Huba and Bentler was not a specific theory of adolescent alcohol or drug use, it was significant in contributing to interactional models of adolescent substance use and to prospective research designs and associated multivariate statistical modeling procedures.

Dynamic Contextual Models

Emerging perspectives of adolescent alcohol use have adopted a developmental-systems orientation in attempting to understand the marked intraindividual variation in alcohol use and alcohol problems across the life course (e.g., Windle & Davies, in press; Zucker, Fitzgerald, & Moses, 1995). These perspectives acknowledge the multifaceted, embedded nature of individual behaviors, such as alcohol use, within a nested domain approach, such as that proposed by Huba and Bentler (1982). That is, individual behavior is simultaneously influenced by a host of intrapersonal, interpersonal, and socialcultural influences. These developmental systems approaches extend the conceptualization of multivariate interactionism in three ways. First, there is much more emphasis on measuring and making inferences about the biological mechanisms and psychosocial processes that contribute to given outcomes. This emphasis encourages forethought to the measurement of key mediators and moderators that are likely to contribute to targeted outcomes (alcohol onset, binge drinking, alcohol disorder). Second, there is an emphasis on bidirectional relations (e.g., "How does parenting affect adolescent drinking, and how does adolescent drinking affect parenting?") and reciprocal feedback processes that maintain, escalate, or terminate alcohol-related behaviors. Third, there is more emphasis on the significance of developmental tasks (e.g., autonomy striving in adolescence) and the disruptive influence of alcohol use on their successful resolution. These emergent developmental perspectives of alcohol use provide vehicles to integrate existing data, theories, and models and may serve a heuristic function of generating hypotheses for subsequent research.

SUMMARY

Alcohol use has a long history in the civilization of humankind. It has been used in important rituals and ceremonies across the ages. In the United States, alcohol use has been quite common among adults and adolescents across history, with legal prohibitions against youthful drinking arising principally after 1930, influenced by a historical trend toward greater state involvement in the public arena. Scientific studies of alcohol use among adolescents over the past 30 years or so have indicated high rates of usage and an earlier age of onset for alcohol use. More recent surveys have also indicated high rates of binge drinking and the manifestation of multiple alcohol problems (e.g., missing school because of drinking, getting into fights because of drinking). Although based on a limited number of local community studies, it has been estimated that between 3% and 32% of adolescents meet lifetime criteria for alcohol disorders. A range of theoretical and conceptual models have been promulgated to explain adolescent alcohol use. These theories and models have been based on individual biogenetic and dispositional features, on socialization influences, on multivariate interactional effects, and on developmental, contextual considerations. The relative adequacy of these theories and models awaits subsequent research in the developing field of adolescent alcohol use.

2

MEASUREMENT AND DIAGNOSIS

Several alternative approaches have been developed to assess alcohol use behaviors among adolescents. These alternative approaches have emerged from differences in the background and disciplinary training of investigators (e.g., sociologists, epidemiologists, psychologists, psychiatrists) and from differences in the targeted behaviors that were the foci of given studies (e.g., alcohol use initiation among national probability samples versus dependency symptoms among inpatient treatment samples). At this time there is no so-called gold standard in the adolescent alcohol studies field with regard to the best assessment protocol. However, there does appear to be a consensus around two important issues. The first is that the measurement of alcohol behaviors in adolescence is multidimensional (Bailey & Rachal, 1993; White & Labouvie, 1989; Windle, 1996; Winters, 1990); the second is that the development of well-validated psychometric measures is lacking and needs to be a priority in the field (Tarter, 1990; Winters, 1990). Furthermore, it should be noted that there is a moderate degree of common use for some survey items across a wide range of studies that facilitates cross-study and cross-cohort comparisons. This chapter provides a presentation of the major alternative assessment approaches that have been used in alcohol studies with adolescents, including a brief description of the protocol, psychometric properties, and applicability and findings in field studies. These measurement procedures include survey questions, screening inventories, and diagnostic interviews.

SURVEY QUESTIONS

Perhaps the most widely used measurement procedure in alcohol studies has been self-report survey questions that have been used in both large-scale national probability studies, such as the MFS (Johnston et al., 1991) and in a multitude of regional and local school-based studies. Because of their widespread use, these survey items and derived scale scores are presented first.

Alcohol Initiation

Research findings have been consistent in indicating a statistically significant association between an earlier age of onset of alcohol use and the subsequent development of more serious problems with alcohol, sometimes including the expression of an alcohol disorder (Barnes & Welte, 1986; von Knorring, Palm, & Anderson, 1985). For example, Barnes and Welte (1986) reported that early alcohol intoxication was a potent predictor of current levels of heavy drinking among adolescents. Age of alcohol initiation has also been of importance to drug sequence or so-called gateway models of substance use that postulate that alcohol use is typically manifested earlier among those adolescents who subsequently progress to marijuana use and then to the use of other illicit drugs, such as heroin or cocaine (Kandel, 1975; Windle, Barnes, & Welte, 1989).

A typical survey item about alcohol initiation is, "At what age did you have your first drink (not just sip) of alcohol," although there have been variations on this question. Whereas this particular question refers to age at the first drink of alcohol, some researchers have focused more on age at the first time drunk, age of first alcohol-related problem (e.g., with parents or with school or legal authorities), or on the location of the drinking episode (e.g., at home with parents or at a party or in a car with peers). Comparative studies have not been conducted across these various items to determine which is the most reliable and most predictive of subsequent alcohol problems, yet all have demonstrated that an earlier, rather than later, onset is associated with more subsequent alcohol-related difficulties.

Although the reported findings across studies have indicated almost universally that an earlier onset of alcohol use is more predictive of problems than is a later onset, there have been some concerns with the reliability of age-of-onset items. In this regard, there are concerns with the (typically) retrospective nature of the items that are subject to the full spectrum of potential unintentional (e.g., faulty recall) and intentional (e.g., social desirability) biases associated with retrospective reports. Bailey, Flewelling, and Rachal (1992) reported on the test-retest reliability of self-reported age of alcohol initiation for a large sample of adolescents (over 5,000 subjects), with a 1-year interval separating occasions of measurement. The findings indicated that 23.2% of the adolescents committed a logical error across these two time points. Examples of logical errors included reporting an age of first use at Time 1 and then reporting never having tried alcohol in lifetime at Time 2 or reporting an age that was inconsistent with the adolescent's current age (e.g., older than the current age). Estimation errors were also computed; these errors did not reflect errors with regard to usage or nonusage but rather with regard to accuracy of the age reported. Over 19% of the adolescents reported an age of initiation at Time 2 that was discrepant with the age reported at Time 1. Of these discrepancies, 46.6% were off by one year, 31.2% by two years, and 22.1% by three or more years. These findings clearly indicate that self-report age-of-alcohol-initiation measures are not perfectly reliable indicators. Nevertheless, they still may be of considerable value to the scientific community in that an earlier alcohol onset during a critical developmental period, such as ages 13 to 16 years may reflect a range of other potential difficulties (e.g., deviant peer relations) and be prognostic of subsequent alcohol problems (Yu & Williford, 1992).

Alcohol Use

The measurement of alcohol consumption may initially appear to be a rather straightforward exercise. However, there are a number of different ways of assessing alcohol use and it is important to note that quite different results may be obtained, contingent on the method selected. For example, Dawson (1998) compared eight different approaches to measuring alcohol use with data from two national surveys of adults. She reported that, contingent on the method used, average daily ethanol consumption ranged from 0.43 ounces to 0.72 ounces (0.50 ounces represents about one alcoholic beverage, i.e., one 12-ounce beer, a 4-ounce glass of wine, or 1.5 ounces of spirits). Converting these figures to a more common metric, the variability in the estimates of average alcohol consumption measured for the past 30 days ranged from 12.90 drinks to 21.60 drinks, contingent on the method of assessment used. The lowest consumption estimates were obtained with two, nonspecific beverage items on the usual frequency and quantity of alcohol use. The highest consumption estimates were obtained with 21 items that included beverage-specific items (separate items for beer, wine, spirits) for frequency and quantity of use, as well as the heaviest episode of use for each beverage type.

The Dawson (1998) study was conducted with adults, but the issues surrounding optimal methods of assessment (e.g., generic number of drinks vs. beverage type specificity), number of survey items, time referent (e.g., past two weeks, past 30 days, past year, lifetime), and the reliability and validity of the method that is used are of equal concern for adult and adolescent assessment. Regarding method of assessment, periodically, there still are reports of adolescent alcohol use based on one or two items (e.g., "How many drinks have you had in the past year?" or "How many days did you drink in the past 30 days? On average, how many drinks did you consume each time that you drank?"), but these are infrequent as they yield measured scores with less fidelity than alternative methods. The questionnaire items in Table 2.1 provide a more typical method for assessing beer use in adolescent (and adult) survey applications. The items request beverage-specific information on the frequency and quantity of beer consumption, as well as the number of binge drinking episodes. The time referents for these survey items are the past 30 days and the past 6 months, though some investigators prefer to supplement this time window with additional, or alternative, time referents for each of the items (e.g., lifetime, past year). Few investigators use the past 2 weeks as a time referent for alcohol use among adolescents because this may not provide a sufficiently sensitive (or reliable) index for typical patterns of adolescent drinking, which may differ based on varying conditions (e.g., parties, access to an automobile); hence, a longer window (e.g., 30 days, past year) is often adopted. The trade-off is that the retrospective reporting of alcohol use (including the specificity of the beverage consumed, the frequency, and the quantity) may decrease in reliability the longer the recall interval. Similar items pertaining to the quantity, frequency, and binge drinking episodes are also commonly requested in survey research regarding wine and spirits.

Issues surrounding the reliability of adolescent self-reports of alcohol and substance use have been studied extensively (National Institute on Drug Abuse [NIDA], 1985) because most existing data are collected via either surveys or interviews, both of which rely on adolescent accounts of their drinking behavior. The findings have been relatively consistent regarding the high reliability of these assessments (e.g., internal consistency; test-retest reliability over short intervals, such as 2 to 4 weeks; e.g., Oetting & Beauvais, 1990; Smith, McCarthy, & Goldman, 1995). For example, Smith et al. reported internal consistency estimates for an alcohol use-drunkenness subscale with a sample of over 400 early adolescents ranging from .92 to .94 for three successive years of assessment, and a test-retest correlation of .89.

Of equal or more concern than the reliability of assessment for adolescent alcohol use has been the validity of the reporting. Alcohol use is an illegal activity for adolescents, and there have been concerns that this may affect reporting toward less use than is actually practiced: undesirable response tendencies may have biased the estimates. The social-desirability response bias notion was consistent with findings in the adult alcohol use literature

TABLE 2.1   Alcohol Use Survey

1. How often did you *usually* have *beer*

   a. in the past 30 days?
   _____ Never
   _____ About once a month
   _____ 2 or 3 days a month
   _____ About once a week
   _____ 2 or 3 days a week
   _____ 4 or 5 days a week
   _____ Every day

   b. in the past 6 months?
   _____ Never
   _____ A few times in past 6 months
   _____ About once a month
   _____ 2 or 3 days a month
   _____ About once a month
   _____ 2 or 3 days a week
   _____ 4 or 5 days a week
   _____ Every day

2. When you had beer, on the average, how much did you *usually* drink

   a. in the past 30 days?

   On an average day when you drank beer, how many beers did you usually drink?

   _____ I drank no beer
   _____ 1 can or bottle
   _____ 2 cans or bottles
   _____ 3 cans or bottles
   _____ 4 cans or bottles
   _____ 5 cans or bottles
   _____ 6 cans or bottles
   _____ 7 cans or bottles
   _____ 8 cans or bottles
   _____ more than 8 cans or bottles
   (Please specify: _____)

   b. in the past 6 months?

   On an average day when you drank beer, how many beers did you usually drink?

   _____ I drank no beer
   _____ 1 can or bottle
   _____ 2 cans or bottles
   _____ 3 cans or bottles
   _____ 4 cans or bottles
   _____ 5 cans or bottles
   _____ 6 cans or bottles
   _____ 7 cans or bottles
   _____ 8 cans or bottles
   _____ more than 8 cans or bottles
   (Please specify: _____)

3. How many times did you drink 5 or more cans or bottles of beer at one time
   (Fill in the number of times)

   a. in the past 30 days?
   ___ ___ ___ times
      number

   b. in the past 6 months?
   ___ ___ ___ times
      number

that indicated that adults tended to underreport their alcohol use and that heavier users tended to be the most flagrant underreporters (Lemmens, Tan, & Knibbe, 1992). Alternative methods have been used to evaluate the validity of adolescent self-reported alcohol use. Wagenaar, Komro, McGovern, Williams, and Perry (1993) used the saliva pipeline procedure with sixth and eighth graders. This procedure involves an experimental manipulation in which the subjects in the pipeline condition are requested to provide a sample of saliva at the beginning of the testing session. They are informed that the saliva will be tested in a laboratory and will provide a biological measure of alcohol use; the control subjects do not provide a saliva sample. Then, all subjects complete questionnaires that include items about alcohol use. The relative rates of self-reported alcohol use are then compared between the two randomly assigned groups (pipeline condition and control groups). Incidentally, saliva samples may be used to detect recent alcohol use (e.g., past 24 hours) prior to metabolism, but they are not a useful measure of alcohol use over longer periods of time (e.g., past 2 weeks); hence, the collection of the saliva samples is intended to "trick" students into believing that there is an independent verification source for their self-reported alcohol use behaviors.

The findings of Wagenaar et al. (1993) were that those students in the pipeline condition reported 5% to 7% higher alcohol use than the control group. However, a further breakdown by grade level (sixth and eighth) and five specific alcohol use items indicated only one statistically significant effect—self-reported lifetime alcohol use was 76% for the pipeline group and 67.7% for the control group among the eighth graders. However, there were no statistically significant differences for sixth or eighth graders across alcohol use items for 7-day, 30-day, or 12-month windows or for binge drinking. These findings were consistent with previous pipeline studies of alcohol use (e.g., Campanelli, Dielman, & Shope, 1987) and suggest that, to the extent that the pipeline condition is an effective perceived verification method, adolescent self-reports are valid.

Another approach to validating adolescent self-reports of alcohol use has been to use collateral informants to evaluate correspondence between adolescent self-reports and informants' reports of alcohol use by the target adolescent. Adolescent drinking often occurs either without parental knowledge or with parental knowledge that their adolescent drinks but with inaccurate information regarding the frequency and quantity of use. Hence, parents are often not useful collateral informants in general population studies. Smith et al. (1995) used peer collateral informants and reported Pearson correlations of .62 between adolescent and collateral reports of the target's typical drinking and drunkenness. Furthermore, both the target adolescent and the peer completed 7-day retrospective diaries of the target's alcohol use; correlations between the adolescent self-reports and the collateral reports were .39 for number of days alcohol was consumed, .62 for total amount of alcohol consumed, and .64 for most alcohol consumed in one day.

As is the case in other domains of child and adolescent psychopathology (e.g., aggression, delinquency, conduct problems, sexual activity, depression, anxiety), adolescent self-reports are an essential component of alcohol use assessment because in some instances, adult raters (parents, teachers, counselors, therapists) do not have access to the data. Adolescent alcohol use most often occurs outside of the parental or school context and with peers. Parents and teachers may have strong suspicions regarding the drinking behavior of adolescents and certainly become aware if there are legal encounters (e.g., alcohol-related crashes) or serious school problems associated with drinking, but typically, they are not useful collateral sources for describing the details (frequency and quantity, alcohol problems) of their adolescents' drinking in general population samples. Hence, it is fortunate that the available evidence suggests that self-reporting by adolescents regarding alcohol use is reasonably reliable and valid.

Heavy Episodic or Binge Drinking

In addition to the measurement of quantity and frequency of alcohol use, there has been increasing interest in the role of heavy, episodic occasions of drinking or the number of times an adolescent drinks until drunk. Because of the largely subjective nature of self-reported drunkenness, heavy episodic drinking has become more frequently used in the literature and has been operationalized to refer to drinking five (or some researchers use six) or more drinks per drinking occasion—for example, in a single evening at a party. In a widely publicized study of alcohol use among college students, Weschler, Davenport, Dowdall, Moeykens, & Castillo (1994) popularized the term *binge drinking* or *binge drinking episodes* to refer to this manifestation of drinking behavior, and this convention is adopted in this book. Note, however, that in this book, the term is used descriptively and does not imply any necessary etiologic corollary, such as with binge eating episodes associated with eating disorders. Nevertheless, the measurement of binge drinking is viewed as important because it represents a drinking style that is significantly correlated with a range of alcohol-related problems (e.g., drinking and driving, risky sexual activity) and is prognostic of subsequent problems with alcohol and in other spheres of life (Schulenberg et al., 1996). Binge drinking is commonly associated with the attainment of legal levels of intoxication (blood alcohol levels greater than or equal to .08) and with self-reported drunkenness. This level of alcohol ingestion may contribute significantly to a loss of motor control, impaired judgment abilities, and reduced inhibitions.

One might mistakenly believe that binge drinking is a relatively uncommon phenomenon until the senior year of high school or is largely postponed until the college or young adulthood years. However, data among even 8th and 10th graders derived from the National Adolescent Student Health

Survey (NASHS; American School Health Association, 1989; also see Windle, 1991) show that the prevalence of binge drinking *in the past two weeks* is over 35% for some subsamples of 8th graders (e.g., Hispanic boys) and over 40% for some subsamples of 10th graders (Hispanic and white boys). Furthermore, even though black boys and black girls show the lowest levels of binge drinking among the 8th and 10th graders, the prevalence is still over 15% among 8th graders and over 25% among 10th graders. Hence, binge drinking is an early-onset characteristic of alcohol use that is variable across ethnic groups and gender but that is self-reported by a large number of early adolescents.

Data for somewhat older adolescents (e.g., high school seniors) are consistent with these data for early adolescents. Findings from the MFS (Johnston et al., 1996) indicated that the prevalence of binge drinking in the past two weeks for high school seniors in the successive years of 1995, 1996, and 1997 was 29.8%, 30.2%, and 31.3%, respectively. Similarly, the prevalence of having been drunk in the past 30 days for these senior classes was 33.2%, 31.3%, and 34.2%, respectively. Parenthetically, it is important to recognize that most school-based, national surveys, such as the NASHS and the MFS, may underestimate the extensiveness of alcohol consumption, alcohol problems, and binge drinking because children and adolescents who drop out of school are not included in these estimates. Higher rates of alcohol and drug use are associated with dropping out of school, and the rates of alcohol and drug use are especially underestimated for some racial or ethnic groups with high rates of dropping out of school (Swaim, Beauvais, Chavez, & Oetting, 1997).

Alcohol Problems

Although alcohol use has been the most frequently studied outcome variable in studies of adolescent drinking behavior, there has been increasing interest in and concern with the extensiveness of alcohol problems among youth. This concern about alcohol problems has gained considerable prominence given that alcohol use is commonly associated with a multitude of problem behaviors (e.g., poor school performance, delinquent activity) and the three most common forms of adolescent morbidity—homicide, suicide, and accidental death. Furthermore, research has indicated that although the correlation between alcohol use and alcohol problems is statistically significant ($r = .45$), there are individual differences associated with the expression of alcohol problems after controlling for levels of alcohol use (Sadava, 1985). For example, Windle and Blane (1989) reported that lower levels of intellectual functioning were predictive of alcohol problems after controlling for level of alcohol use. Similarly, the findings of Barnes and Welte (1986) indicated that black adolescents, relative to white adolescents, had more alcohol-related problems at comparable levels of alcohol consumption. It is also important to note that adolescent alcohol problems are a significant public health concern because of the multiple associated societal costs associated with adolescent accidents, violence, and other disinhibitory behaviors (e.g., vandalism, school dropout), as well as treatment costs. Furthermore, there are some investigators who believe that a portion of the preventive intervention continuum of services should be focused on harm reduction end points (i.e., eliminating or mitigating the alcohol-related problems) rather than, or in addition to, abstinence-based or alcohol-reduction approaches. In essence, the argument is that current preventive interventions have had limited success in reducing adolescent alcohol use and that a focus on the adverse consequences (e.g., fatal crashes, suicides, dropping out of school) may benefit the public health of all members of society.

The more comprehensive measurement of alcohol problems among adolescents is a relatively recent occurrence, as many early studies focused exclusively on alcohol consumption or, at most, included four or five items pertinent to alcohol problems (Donovan & Jessor, 1978). The Rutgers Health and Human Development Project developed a unidimensional, 23-item measure titled the Rutgers Alcohol Problem Index (RAPI; White & Labouvie, 1989). The content of items from the RAPI included alcohol-related problems at school (e.g., not able to do homework or study for a test), interpersonal difficulties (e.g., relatives avoided you) and aggression (e.g., had a fight, argument, or bad feelings with a friend), and alcohol disorder symptoms (e.g., tried to cut down or quit drinking). An internal consistency estimate of .92 was indicated for the RAPI and correlations between RAPI and a measure of alcohol use intensity ranged from .20 to .57 for adolescents at ages 12, 15, and 18 (higher correlations were indicated for older adolescents).

Windle (1996) also used a measure referred to as the Alcohol Problem Index (API) to measure alcohol-related problems among adolescents. The 13 items that compose this unidimensional index are provided in Table 2.2. These data indicate that a high percentage of adolescents reported the occurrence of alcohol-related problems during the 6-month window referenced for each item. Almost 50% of these adolescents reported doing things while consuming alcohol that they regretted the next day, and over 25% of girls and 33% of boys reported passing out from drinking at least once in the past 6 months. Furthermore, indicators of potentially significant alcohol-disordered behaviors were reported for a substantial minority of these ado-

TABLE 2.2   Alcohol Problems Index: Frequency of Item Endorsement
Among Those Who Drink

	Percentage Endorsing Affirmative Response			
Item	Total N	Boys	Girls	$\chi^2(1\ df)$
1. Drank before or during school	12.1	16.6	8.5	12.61**
2. Missed school because of drinking	8.9	11.2	7.1	4.05*
3. Had a fight with parents about your drinking	16.1	19.3	13.4	5.36*
4. Did things while you were drinking that you regretted the next day	47.4	49.9	45.4	1.59
5. Thought about cutting down on your drinking	24.0	30.2	18.9	14.16**
6. Got drunk or high from alcohol several days in a row	28.3	36.8	21.4	23.42**
7. Passed out from drinking	29.1	33.1	25.8	5.10*
8. Had a fight with your girlfriend or boyfriend about your drinking	15.9	16.1	15.8	0.01
9. Got into a fight or heated argument with someone you didn't know while drinking	16.1	25.1	8.7	40.21**
10. Got into trouble with the law (other than driving-related) while drinking	6.4	11.2	2.4	25.75**
11. Drank alone	21.6	25.3	18.5	5.61*
12. Drank alcohol to get rid of a hangover	7.2	8.7	6.0	2.20
13. Drank to forget your troubles	36.9	34.9	38.5	1.16

NOTE: Abstainers were excluded from these analyses. Time referent for alcohol problems was the past 6 months. Total number of subjects was 695 (321 boys, 374 girls).
*$p < 0.05$.
**$p < 0.01$.

lescents, such as more than 21% drinking alone (adolescent alcohol use is often a peer group activity) and more than 7% drinking to get over a hangover. These findings regarding the high frequency of alcohol-related problems among adolescents are consistent with prior research (Bailey & Rachal, 1993; White & Labouvie, 1989) and a useful source of data about alcohol-related behaviors beyond alcohol consumption.

Various combinations of alcohol use and alcohol-related problems have also been used to form typologies to better account for the heterogeneity of adolescent drinking. For example, Donovan and Jessor (1978) defined adolescent problem drinkers with regard to either frequency of intoxication or on the number of alcohol-related interpersonal and adverse social consequences. Rachal, Hubbard, Williams, and Tuchfeld (1976) also developed a typology that similarly classified problem drinkers on the basis of frequency of intoxication and adverse social consequences associated with drinking. Windle (1996) used multiple criteria to identify five monotonically graded subgroups of adolescent drinkers—abstainers, light drinkers (consumed at least 1 but less than 10 drinks in the past 30 days), moderate drinkers (consumed at least 10 but less than 45 drinks in the past 30 days), heavy drinkers (consumed at least 45 drinks in the past 30 days *or* consumed six or more drinks on at least three occasions in the past 30 days), and problem drinkers (same alcohol use criteria as heavy drinkers *plus* five or more alcohol-related problems in the past 6 months).

Convergent and discriminant validity was reported for the five subgroups identified by Windle (1996) as they differed significantly on a range of theoretically important dimensions. For example, problem drinkers differed significantly from heavy drinkers (and the other subgroups) in that they reported more childhood behavior problems (e.g., symptoms of conduct disorder and attentional deficit hyperactivity disorder), a higher prevalence of paternal alcoholism, and a higher percentage of friends who used illicit drugs; they drank more often to cope with stressors; and they exhibited more disinhibitory behavior while drinking (e.g., more sexually forward, less likely to use protective devices during sexual encounters). Across a 1-year interval, there was evidence of both stability and change across these five drinking categories, as over 50% of problem drinkers remained similarly classified as problem drinkers, whereas only 38% of moderate drinkers remained similarly classified. These data provided support for both stability and change in adolescent drinking behavior across this 1-year interval.

Identifying subgroups of adolescent drinkers is of clinical importance in that such subgroup distinctions may be important in terms of providing a continuum of health care and education. That is, universal programs that emphasize abstinence or peer refusal skills may be relevant for some adolescents (e.g., current abstainers and perhaps light and moderate drinkers) but are not likely to be very successful with adolescent heavy and problem drinkers. Focused or supplemental intervention programs for heavy-drinking and problem-drinking adolescents may require more intensive and extensive interventions (e.g., booster sessions) to facilitate health promotion objectives. Subtypes of adolescent drinkers may also provide significant information on etiology, taxonomy, developmental course, and treatment outcomes for alternative patterns of adolescent alcohol use. Further inquiry into the causal dynamics of problem-drinking adolescents is also needed to evaluate what interventions may be successful with these young people, for whom heavy drinking is associated with a range of adverse consequences for both the adolescent and the public at large.

SCREENING MEASURES

The increasing recognition of the pervasiveness of adolescent alcohol and drug use has spawned the emergence of a wide range of screening measures (e.g., Leccese & Waldron, 1994). In a report issued by the Center for Substance Abuse Treatment (McLellan & Dembo, 1993), the importance of screening for adolescent substance use was emphasized with regard to short-term and long-term objectives (e.g., short-term: early identification, cost-effective referrals for needed services; long-term: reduce long-term care needs, reduce burden on the criminal justice system, lessen long-term care costs). Furthermore, the usefulness of screening for adolescent substance use problems was emphasized for a range of contexts and institutions (e.g., schools, hospitals, detention centers, offices of pediatricians) in which the education and health care communities intermingle with adolescents.

The adolescent screening measures that have been developed are not designed to provide clinical diagnoses of alcohol and other substance abuse disorders but rather to provide a relatively quick assessment of current substance use practices or to provide a broader, more holistic assessment of adolescent interpersonal resources (e.g., family relations), health and education background, previous contact with medical and legal facilities, and substance use practices. Some of the existing adolescent screening measures focus exclusively on alcohol use, although the majority focus more broadly on all substances of abuse (e.g., marijuana, cocaine, solvents). Many of these measures rely on adolescent self-report (and in some instances, parental) questionnaires, whereas others involve semistructured interviews. Several screening measures that vary in terms of their scope are briefly discussed now. (For more extensive reviews, see Leccese & Waldron, 1994; McClellan & Dembo, 1993; NIDA, 1994; Winters, 1990).

The Adolescent Drinking Inventory: Drinking and You (ADI; Harrell, Sowder, & Kapsak, 1988; Harrell & Wirtz, 1989) is a 24-item standardized instrument used by clinicians or counselors (without specialized training in substance abuse assessment) to assist them in their decisions about referring adolescents for further alcohol evaluation. The ADI measures the possible impact of adolescent alcohol use on daily functioning in four domains: loss of control (e.g., frequent intoxication), social symptoms (e.g., difficulties in interpersonal relationships due to drinking), psychological indicators (e.g., drinking to cope with feelings of loneliness or depression), and physical symptoms (e.g., memory problems and tolerance). Scores for these four domains are highly correlated (in excess of .70), and reliability estimates have been high (Cronbach's alpha = .96; 2-week test-retest correlation was .78). Clinician ratings of severity of drinking problems for 264 adolescents referred for evaluation were highly correlated with scores on the ADI (r's ranged from .64 to .71 for the four domain scores). The four domain scores accounted for 55% of the variance in the severity ratings of clinicians (Harrell & Wirtz, 1989).

The Personal Experience Screening Inventory (PESQ; Winters, 1992) is an 18-item self-report measure designed to assess the need for referral for more in-depth evaluation. Each item is rated along a four-point scale with response options "never," "once or twice," "sometimes," and "often." Sample items include "How often have you used alcohol or drugs secretly, so nobody would know that you were using?" and "In order to get or pay for alcohol or other drugs, how often have you sold drugs?" Winters reported that one dominant principal component accounted for interitem correlations of the PESQ, and coefficient alpha was equal to or exceeded .90 for adolescent samples of boys and girls. Last, the PESQ was reasonably sensitive in predicting alcohol and drug abuse referrals that had been based on a much more comprehensive clinical protocol. Note that this screening measure does not distinguish between severity of alcohol or drug use; this is by design as it is a screening measure of substance use. For a more comprehensive assessment, Henly and Winters (1989) have proposed the use of the Personal Experiences Inventory, which includes alcohol- and drug-specific behaviors, DSM-III-R (APA, 1987) diagnosis, and expanded domain evaluation (e.g., family pathology, peer substance use).

The Problem-Oriented Screening Instrument for Teenagers (POSIT; Rahdert, 1991) is a self-administered 139-item questionnaire to be completed by adolescents 12 to 19 years old. The POSIT assesses 10 functional areas: (a) alcohol and drug use and abuse, (b) physical health, (c) mental health, (d) family relations, (e) peer relations, (f) educational status, (g) vocational status, (h) social skills, (i) leisure-recreation, and (j) aggressive behavior. Cutoff points are derived for each of the functional areas, and scores beyond a given threshold are indicative of referral and additional diagnostic evaluation. The POSIT was designed for use by a variety of health professionals, including school personnel, court personnel, medical care providers, and staff members at adolescent alcohol and drug abuse centers.

The Drug Use Screening Inventory-Revised (DUSI-R; Tarter, 1990; Tarter & Hegedus, 1991) is a 159-item self-administered instrument for individuals between 11 years of age and adulthood. The reading level for this self-administered measure is a sixth-grade vocabulary and a fifth-grade reading level; this may be of importance in some settings where low reading levels may preclude using self-administered forms if the reading level of the form is too high. The DUSI-R measures the 10 life problem areas of (a) substance use behavior, (b) behavior patterns, (c) health status, (d) psychiatric disorder, (e) social competence, (f) family system, (g) school adjustment, (h) work, (i) peer relationships, and (j) leisure and recreation. Alternative scores may be derived from the DUSI-R, including an Absolute Problem Density score for each of the 10 problem areas and a composite Summary Problem Index by summing across the 10 problem domains. Each score represents the severity of problems in the respective domains.

The average internal consistency estimate for the DUSI-R across the 10 problem domains for a sample of 191 youths with alcohol and drug abuse disorders was .78 (Tarter, 1990; Tarter & Hegedus, 1991). The validity of several of the domain scores has been supported, as the Substance Use Behavior problem density score correlated .72 with the number of substance abuse symptoms from a DSM-III-R (APA, 1987) checklist, and the problem density score of the Psychiatric Disorder scale correlated .65 with the total number of symptoms reported on the Kiddie-Schizophrenia and Affective Disorders Scale (Puig-Antich & Chambers, 1978). The DUSI-R is available in both standard paper-and-pencil and computer-administered formats (Tarter, 1990).

This sampling of screening measures for adolescent alcohol and drug use illustrates that initial progress in this area has been made. A strength of these measures is the recognition of the need to assess multiple domains of functioning to facilitate an appropriate evaluation of problems, resources, and service needs. By identifying both the severity and range of problems, better matches may be made between client needs and the continuum of treatment and service offerings. Efforts were also made to limit the amount of time to complete these screening measures and to make them self-administered. These features are important in many education, health, and penal contexts where lengthy interview protocols by professionally trained staff members are not feasible. Despite the considerable progress on screening measures in recent years, research needs remain high in this area. Additional information is needed, for instance, on the validity of some of these measures and their utility in evaluating treatment progress, identifying sensitive problems, and addressing issues of underreporting and misreporting. In addition, research is needed to evaluate the efficacy of these screening measures to refer clients to the appropriate treatment and service settings and to evaluate their perceived usefulness to health care practitioners.

CLINICAL DIAGNOSIS
OF ALCOHOL DISORDERS

There has been a substantial increase in the number of screening measures for substance use among adolescents in recent years and a focus on the identification and reliable measurement of multiple dimensions of alcohol-related behaviors. However, there has been much less effort directed toward systematic, empirical studies of formal diagnostic criteria associated with DSM-derived alcohol disorders among teens. A partial explanation for the limited number of studies on this topic is that the clinical diagnosis of alcohol disorders among adolescents is a controversial topic. For example, it has been argued that the clinical symptoms and diagnostic criteria used to define alcohol disorders among adults are not necessarily the most appropriate for analyzing and diagnosing alcohol disorders among adolescents (Brown, Mott, & Myers, 1990; Bukstein & Kaminer, 1994; Winters, 1990). That is, given our current knowledge of adolescent and adult drinking practices and associated consequences, it has been questioned as to whether these symptoms and criteria are optimal, or even adequate, to assess alcohol disorders among adolescents.

Table 2.3 provides the symptoms and criteria for Substance-Related Disorders based on the Diagnostic and Statistical Manual, version IV (DSM-IV; APA, 1994). The symptoms and criteria for Substance Dependence are characterized by co-occurring cognitive, behavioral, and physiological symptoms that persist despite the problematic nature of the expressed symptoms. The prolonged use of substances such as alcohol frequently results in increased tolerance, withdrawal, and compulsive alcohol use. Tolerance in the consumption of alcohol can occur when perhaps 12 to 14 drinks are required to attain the same "high" as was previously achieved with 5 to 6 drinks. Thus, individuals may initiate heavier alcohol use with the intent of getting high and feeling very much in control of their consumption. However, across time, more and more alcohol may be required to achieve the same desired state. In addition, cognitive and physiological withdrawal symptoms may occur when efforts are made to reduce or cease alcohol use. Some individuals respond to the unpleasant feelings associated with alcohol withdrawal (nausea, headaches, tremors) by consuming alcohol in the morning and continually using it throughout the day. Such drinking patterns typically create difficulties in

TABLE 2.3   Diagnostic and Statistical Manual of Mental Disorders
(DSM-IV) Criteria for Substance Disorders

A. Criteria for Substance Dependence—A maladaptive pattern of substance use, leading to
clinically significant impairment or distress, as manifested by three (or more) of the
following, occurring at any time in the same 12-month period:
  (1) Tolerance as defined by either of the following:
      (a) A need for markedly increased amounts of the substance to achieve intoxication
          or desired effect
      (b) Markedly diminished effect with continued use of the same amount of the
          substance
  (2) Withdrawal, as manifested by either of the following:
      (a) The characteristic withdrawal syndrome for the substance (refer to Criteria A and
          B of the criteria sets for Withdrawal from the specific substances)
      (b) The same (or a closely related) substance is taken to relieve or avoid withdrawal)
  (3) The substance is often taken in larger amounts or over a longer period than was
      intended
  (4) There is a persistent desire or unsuccessful efforts to cut down or control substance
      use
  (5) A great deal of time is spent in activities necessary to obtain the substance (e.g.,
      visiting multiple doctors or driving long distances), use the substance (e.g.,
      chain-smoking), or recover from its effects
  (6) Important social, occupational, or recreational activities are given up or reduced
      because of substance use
  (7) The substance use is continued despite knowledge of having a persistent or recurrent
      physical or psychological problem that is likely to have been caused or exacerbated
      by the substance (e.g., current cocaine use despite recognition of cocaine-induced
      depression, or continued drinking despite recognition that an ulcer was made worse
      by alcohol consumption)

      Specify if:
          With physiological dependence: Evidence of tolerance or withdrawal
              (i.e., either Item 1 or 2 is present)
          Without physiological dependence: No evidence of tolerance or withdrawal
              (i.e., neither Item 1 nor 2 is present)
B. Criteria for Substance Abuse
  (1) A maladaptive pattern of substance use leading to clinically significant impairment or
      distress, as manifested by one (or more) of the following, occurring within a
      12-month period:
      (a) Recurrent substance use resulting in a failure to fulfill major role obligations at
          work, school, or home (e.g., repeated absences or poor work performance related
          to substance use; substance-related absences, suspensions, or expulsions from
          school; neglect of children or household)
      (b) Recurrent substance use in situations in which it is physically hazardous (e.g.,
          driving an automobile or operating a machine when impaired by substance use)
      (c) Recurrent substance-related legal problems (e.g., arrests for substance-related
          disorderly conduct)
      (d) Continued substance use despite having persistent or recurrent social or
          interpersonal problems caused or exacerbated by the effects of the substance
          (e.g., arguments with spouse about consequences of intoxication, physical fights)
  (2) The symptoms have never met the criteria for Substance Dependence for this class of
      substance

SOURCE: Reprinted with permission from the *Diagnostic and Statistical Manual of Mental Disorders,
Fourth Edition.* Copyright 1994 American Psychiatric Association.

many spheres of life (e.g., family, occupation), and alcohol may become the obsessive foreground feature in a person's life rather than an optional background feature that characterizes the recreational use of alcohol. Criteria for alcohol dependence require a maladaptive pattern of use accompanied by three or more of the criteria listed in Table 2.3. Physiological dependence is indicated if either Criterion 1 (tolerance) or Criterion 2 (withdrawal) are presenting symptoms. The criteria for Substance Abuse are provided in the lower section of Table 2.3. The abuse criteria do not include tolerance and withdrawal but do include persistent alcohol use accompanied by major adverse social consequences, such as failure in major family and occupational roles, or physically hazardous activities (e.g., repetitive heavy drinking and driving), and alcohol-influenced interpersonal problems, such as arguments with spouse or physical fights. An alcohol abuse disorder diagnosis may be met by the manifestation of one or more of these criteria in the past 12 months.

Adequacy of Adult Criteria for Adolescents

Concerns have been raised about the comparability of some of the criteria and symptoms for adolescents and adults. For example, the long-term duration of drinking required to manifest certain medical complications (alcoholic liver cirrhosis, serious neurological impairment) and some dependency symptoms (e.g., withdrawal symptoms), which presumably require time for cellular adaptations to alcohol and related dependency processes (e.g., kindling) to occur, are not applicable given the relatively short span of drinking among adolescents. Brown et al. (1990) have also raised issues based on their studies of adolescents in chemical dependency programs. They concluded that adolescents in treatment are quite distinct from adults in treatment. Specifically, they noted that adolescents in treatment are much more likely to be polysubstance users and abusers and to have higher rates of psychiatric comorbidity than adults in treatment settings. Furthermore, Brown et al. noted that stressors are identified as precipitants of relapse among adults, but social drinking motives (using substances with friends) are more likely to be relapse precipitants among adolescents. These differences between adolescents and adults create potential problems in diagnosis to the extent that symptom manifestations and associated problems may index different pathological processes, with different implications for treatment.

Two recent studies have focused on an evaluation of the formal DSM-IV (APA, 1994) criteria for alcohol disorders with adolescent samples. Martin, Kaczynski, Maisto, Bukstein, and Moss (1995) used a modified version of the Structured Clinical Interview for the DSM with a sample of 181 adolescents (91 boys, 90 girls). Approximately 50% were recruited from alcohol and substance abuse treatment programs and 50% from community advertisements. Subsequent to a thorough analysis of the symptom data, the authors concluded that there was general support for the alcohol dependence concept as measured via DSM-IV (APA, 1994) criteria (there was moderate to high symptom covariation), but that in contrast to prior findings with adult samples, some symptoms (e.g., medical problems, withdrawal symptoms) were quite infrequently expressed. Furthermore, tolerance, which typically has high specificity with regard to alcohol dependence among adults, had low specificity with regard to alcohol dependence for this adolescent sample. Martin et al. (1995) also reported that several alcohol-related problems (blackouts, craving, risky sexual behavior) not identified as symptoms of DSM-IV (APA, 1994) alcohol dependence disorder may be highly prevalent among adolescents; this does not necessarily suggest that these problems are unique to adolescents, however.

Winters, Latimer, and Stinchfield (in press) compared results using DSM-III-R (APA, 1987) and DSM-IV (APA, 1994) criteria with a sample of 722 adolescents (63% boys, 37% girls) recruited from drug clinics in the Minneapolis-St. Paul area. The ADI (Winters & Henly, 1993) was used to assess disorders using each of the two DSM systems. Similar to the findings by Martin et al. (1995), there was a low rate for DSM-III-R withdrawal symptoms (6.4%), and tolerance had a substantially lower correlation with alcohol dependence than in prior studies with adults. Thus, the findings from the studies of Martin et al. and Winters et al. (in press) converge in suggesting that the current diagnostic criteria for alcohol disorders, which had been developed on the basis of symptoms of adult patients, bears increased scrutiny for its comprehensiveness and adequacy to assess adolescent alcohol disorders.

Of further note regarding the Winters et al. (in press) comparative study of DSM-III-R (APA, 1987) and DSM-IV (APA, 1994) criteria, there were shifts in cases across the two systems, with a fair portion of DSM-III-R alcohol dependent adolescents reclassified as alcohol abusers and a few cases meeting alcohol abuse criteria for the DSM-IV system that were not classified as having a disorder under the DSM-III-R system. These reclassifications are consistent with changes in the DSM-IV criteria for alcohol abuse and alcohol dependence. However, there is concern that the one-symptom threshold for alcohol abuse may contribute to a quite heterogeneous group of DSM-IV alcohol abusers; this heterogeneity may not be unique to adolescents but may have a differentially greater impact on prevalence rates for adolescents versus adults because of the higher rate of binge drinking episodes among adolescents, differences in drinking locations, variability in drinking and judging level of intoxication (e.g., prior to driving), and different rates of maturity surrounding drinking behavior.

The two previous studies (Martin et al., 1995; Winters et al., in press) of formal diagnostic criteria for alcohol disorders among adolescents provide initial evidence to substantiate the concerns raised in the research literature (e.g., Brown et al., 1990; Winters, 1990) about the adequacy of the current adult symptoms and criteria. Some of the symptoms (e.g., some withdrawal symptoms) are likely to be manifested at a much lower rate among adolescents, and other potential symptoms (blackouts, craving, risky sexual behavior) are not currently part of the diagnostic criteria. A comprehensive study of symptom reports among alcohol-abusing adolescents collected via adolescents themselves and health care providers (e.g., counselors, pediatricians) has not been conducted. These initial findings support the need for a more systematic method to evaluate symptoms and criteria for adolescent alcohol disorders.

SUMMARY

A number of distinctive dimensions have been identified to characterize adolescent drinking behaviors and disorders, such as frequency and quantity of alcohol consumption and alcohol-related problems. Recent attempts to identify the salient dimensions have been in agreement with the need to conceptualize and measure these behaviors within a multidimensional framework (e.g., Bailey & Rachal, 1993; Harrell & Wirtz, 1989; Windle, 1996; Winters, 1990), though different but overlapping dimensions have been proposed. As described in this chapter, different measures of alcohol behaviors may provide different information and may be differentially related to specific behaviors. For example, percentage of lifetime users of alcohol may provide useful information for federal or state surveillance purposes, but for purposes of identifying at-risk adolescents for intervention programs, binge drinking episodes would be a better measure. In both the popular and scientific press, adolescent alcohol use is often described as if it is a unitary dimension. However, from a basic and applied research perspective, the identification of different subgroups of adolescent alcohol users (e.g., heavy drinkers vs. problem drinkers) will focus attention on issues related to differences in etiology, taxonomy, developmental course, and treatment outcome of the various subtypes.

The inclusion of multiple dimensions of alcohol behaviors and the wider spectrum of personal and social resources and deficits is being incorporated into screening measures for adolescent substance use. Screening measures have a significant role to play in the assessment and evaluation of treatment referral among the many health professionals and institutional settings that come into contact with alcohol and drug abusing adolescents. Although a positive feature of many of the existing screening measures is the attempt to be more comprehensive, there is also a need to develop shorter screening measures to accommodate some settings (e.g., pediatricians' offices, adolescent trauma patient interviews). Issues surrounding the adequacy of adult disorder criteria for adolescents remains controversial. The initial empirical data (Martin et al., 1995; Winters et al., in press) on this issue highlight the need for greater scrutiny and research on adolescent alcohol disorder taxonomy and classification.

3

RISK AND
PROTECTIVE FACTORS

Although alcohol use among adolescents constitutes an illegal activity according to criminal law, the vast majority of adolescents have used alcohol at least once prior to their senior year of high school. Given the widespread use of alcohol during adolescence, an array of important research questions have focused on what factors increase risk for the more troubling aspects of adolescent alcohol use, such as early onset, escalation to frequent high levels of drinking, alcohol-associated problems (e.g., poor school performance, conflict with parents, violence, and driving under the influence), and manifestations of alcohol dependency symptoms. A broad range of risk factors have been identified that do increase the risk for alcohol use behaviors among children and adolescents (e.g., Hawkins, Catalano, & Miller, 1992). No single factor has emerged as omnipotent in the prediction of adolescent alcohol-related behaviors. Rather, constellations of factors tend to co-occur in the prediction of problematic outcomes.

More recent research has also focused on the identification of factors that mitigate or eliminate risk for the expression of problematic alcohol use behaviors; such factors are referred to as *protective factors* (Garmezy & Rutter,1983; Werner & Smith,1982). In this chapter, findings regarding risk and protective factors for adolescent alcohol use behaviors are summarized. These findings are important because (a) they assist in providing a conceptual framework for understanding the multiple, time-varying influences of factors that contribute to phenotypically distinct alcohol-related outcomes (e.g., alcohol onset, escalation, termination) and (b) they provide important information to guide preventive interventions.

Alternative schemes may be used to categorize risk and protective factors. For instance, some risk and protective factors are alcohol-specific (e.g., alcohol expectancies, physiological flushing response to alcohol), whereas

39

others generalize to other emotional and behavioral problems (e.g., family conflict, poor coping skills). The general scheme adopted for presentation in this chapter is based on a systems-oriented social-ecological model to facilitate potential linkages to the preventive intervention research that is provided in the next chapter. Factors have been divided into the four interrelated domains of individual (biological and psychological), peer, family, and social-community factors

INDIVIDUAL FACTORS

Family History of Alcoholism

A positive family history of alcoholism has been associated with between a fourfold and ninefold risk of alcoholism in male offspring (Cloninger, Bohman, & Sigvardsson, 1981; Russell, 1990). That is, sons of male alcoholics are between 4 and 9 times as likely to express an alcohol disorder as the sons of men who are not alcoholics. These findings have been supported via adoptee and twin research design, and are consistent with family resemblance studies in supporting a genetic, intergenerational association for the inheritance of alcohol disorders (Heath,1995; McGue, 1994).

The magnitude of risk associated with a positive family history of alcoholism has spawned a considerable amount of research in recent years, with a general focus on the biological mechanisms (e.g., biogenetic underpinnings) and psychosocial processes (e.g., family conflict and violence) that underlie this heightened risk (for more extensive reviews of this burgeoning literature, see Sher, 1991; Windle & Searles, 1990; Windle & Tubman, in press). The derivation of heritability estimates from several twin studies has yielded estimates ranging from 30% to 70% for an alcohol disorder, though the confidence intervals surrounding these estimates are substantial and preclude any definitive, well-bounded point estimate of heritability (Heath, Sluske, & Madden, 1997). Nevertheless, behavioral geneticists have proceeded to address important substantive issues regarding the generalizability of potential genetic influences for women as well as men (Heath et al., 1997; Kendler, Heath, Neale, Kessler, & Eaves, 1992) and the significance of gene-environment interactions and correlations to account for the heterogeneous outcomes among children of alcoholics. Furthermore, there is a current focus on the genetic contributions to specific, alcohol-related phenotypes (e.g., tolerance, severity of dependence) that will likely yield important information on genetic liability.

There have also been some initial efforts to identify genetic influences (e.g., susceptibility loci) at the molecular genetic level to account for the expression of alcohol disorders. The most well-studied susceptibility locus is among individuals of Japanese, Chinese, or Korean ancestry and the contribution of a polymorphism at the ALDH2 locus (Thomasson, Crabb, & Edenberg,1993). This genetic polymorphism is ultimately involved in a primary metabolic pathway that leads to the oxidation and elimination of ethanol in the liver. Individual variation exists in the activity of aldehyde dehydrogenase (ALDH) among Asians, with low levels of activity associated with a flushing response when alcohol is consumed (due to a reduction in the rate of elimination, elevated acetaldehyde levels, and acute toxic reactions), which is quite unpleasant. This genetically influenced flushing response is associated with reduced alcohol use and alcoholic risk (Thomasson et al., 1993) and thus functions as a protective factor. However, as summarized by McGue (1995), despite the fact that the ALDH2 allele is similar in population frequency among Japanese, Chinese, and Koreans, the prevalence of alcoholism across these groups is quite diverse, with Japanese and Chinese among the lowest in the world and Korean men among the highest (Helzer, Canino, & Yeh, 1990). Hence, even when there is solid support for a genetically influenced characteristic of alcohol behavior, it is evident that cultural (environmental) factors must also be considered to account for the variation in outcomes.

A second susceptibility loci for alcoholism has been implicated via the dopaminergic system and DRD2 gene (Blum et al., 1990). However, despite considerable excitement and enthusiasm over the initial reporting of the significance of the DRD2 gene, subsequent research has been mixed, at best, with regard to replicating the associations reported by Blum et al. (for brief reviews, see Heath et al., 1997; McGue, 1995; Noble, 1998). Furthermore, no linkage was found between markers of DRD2 and alcoholism in one of the positive association studies that had been reported (Parsian et al., 1991). Findings from a large-scale study referred to as the Collaborative Study of the Genetics of Alcoholism have provided evidence of susceptibility loci for alcohol dependence on chromosomes 1 and 7 and modest evidence for chromosome 2 (Reich et al., 1998). Subsequent research on these and other potentially identifiable susceptibility loci are likely to increase substantially in the coming years. To the extent that such susceptibility loci are trait markers for alcoholism, it is possible that they may be identified in childhood and adolescence and may facilitate the study of the etiology and time course of alcohol-related behaviors and provide valuable information to guide more successful preventive interventions, especially among high risk adolescents.

Temperament and Personality

Temperament attributes have been defined in numerous ways, but there is a general consensus that there is individual variation in temperament style and that such attributes reflect early onset (e.g., at birth, during infancy), genetically influenced, relatively stable aspects of behavior that are involved in emotional reactivity and the regulation of behavior (Kohnstamm, Bates, & Rothbart, 1989). Several studies have indicated significant associations between temperament and alcohol use among adolescents (Blackson,Tarter, Loeber, Ammerman & Windle, 1996; Tarter, 1988; Tubman & Windle, 1995; Wills, Windle, & Cleary, 1998). For example, Tubman and Windle (1995) reported that, both concurrently and prospectively over a 1-year interval, a more difficult temperament (defined as higher activity level, lower task orientation, inflexibility, a withdrawal orientation, biological arrhythmicity, and low positive mood) predicted higher levels of alcohol problems among adolescents. Tarter has developed and provided preliminary support for a model in which a more difficult temperament is inherited by male offspring of substance-abusing fathers, which in turn contributes to a multifactorial liability for substance abuse disorders among the offspring. Blackson et al. (1996) reported findings that more difficult temperament styles expressed by both substance-abusing fathers and their male offspring were associated with more conflict between fathers and sons and the earlier involvement of sons in deviant peer networks.

In contrast to these studies supporting a difficult temperament as a risk factor for the development of adverse, alcohol-related behaviors, Werner and Smith (1982) reported how temperament may function as a protective factor for high risk groups. In their influential longitudinal Kauai study of low-SES children of alcohol-abusing parents, Werner and Smith reported that a cuddly, affectionate temperament style in infancy and early childhood was associated with a decreased risk for alcohol-related and other adverse outcomes in adolescence and adulthood. The explanation offered for these findings was that such children elicited more frequent and stronger social and emotional support from their environmental contexts. This support, in turn, contributed to the development of age-appropriate social and cognitive skills that facilitated normative development and was perpetuated across the life course. The concept of *goodness of fit* (Lerner & Lerner, 1983) accommodates these seemingly differently valenced findings of Werner and Smith in comparison with those of others (Tarter, 1988; Tubman & Windle, 1995), in that temperament attributes are viewed as relational—influenced by and influencing their physical and social contexts. As such, individual variation in temperament may contribute to negative or positive interactional cycles that are perpetuated across time and setting, contingent on the individual characteristics and contextual demands involved.

In addition to research demonstrating significant associations between temperament dimensions and adolescent alcohol use, there have also been some studies conducted on personality dispositions and adolescent alcohol use that have supported significant associations. For example, there have been consistently positive associations between sensation seeking and higher levels of adolescent alcohol use (Zuckerman, 1994). Cloninger, Sigvardsson, and Bohman (1988) reported that childhood (age 11 years) personality characteristics of high novelty seeking, high reward dependence, and low harm avoidance predicted subsequent alcohol abuse (also see Wills et al., 1998). Other studies have reported statistically significant correlations between aggression and features of behavioral undercontrol (delinquent activity, impulsivity, difficulty inhibiting responses) and more serious levels of adolescent alcohol use (Sher, 1994). The available evidence on temperament and personality associations with adolescent alcohol use strongly suggests that some of these attributes are influential in the expression of adolescent alcohol-related behaviors. Furthermore, many of the attributes appear to share a core commonality associated with low disinhibitory control and behavioral dysregulation.

Childhood Behavior Problems

Several long-term, prospective studies have supported an association between externalizing childhood behavior problems (physical aggression and violence, symptoms of conduct disorder) and the subsequent development of early-onset alcohol problems and the expression of alcohol disorders in adulthood (McCord & McCord, 1960; Robins, 1966; Vaillant, 1983; Zucker & Gomberg, 1986). Moreover, other more short-term prospective studies have yielded significant associations between childhood undersocialized aggression and hyperactivity and higher levels of alcohol use among adolescents (August, Stewart, & Holmes, 1983; Blouin, Bornstein, & Trites, 1978).

In a recent prospective study of 755 6-year old boys, Dobkin, Tremblay, Masse, and Vitaro (1995) reported that disruptive behaviors (fighting, hyperactivity, oppositional behaviors) measured at age 6 years significantly predicted having been drunk or using other drugs—or both—prior to age 14 years. Similarly, in a separate prospective study of children, Johnson, Arria, Borges, Ialongo, and Anthony (1995) reported that earlier, unsanctioned alcohol use (i.e., without parental permission) was associated with more conduct problem behaviors by ages 10 to 12 years and by a more accelerated growth of these conduct problems across the transition from late childhood to early adolescence. In addition, these relationships generalized across boys and girls.

In a study of 166 adolescents (99 boys and 67 girls) in treatment for alcohol and drug abuse, Brown, Gleghorn, Schuckit, Myers, and Mott (1996) reported that 47% met DSM-III-R criteria for conduct disorder. The occurrence of conduct disorder among this sample of treated adolescents was related to a poorer clinical course in a 2-year, posttreatment follow-up study. Treated adolescents with a clinical diagnosis of conduct disorder, were involved in higher levels of alcohol use (more drinking days per month), more alcohol problems, and more alcohol withdrawal symptoms during the 2-year follow-up period, compared to treated adolescents without conduct disorder. In addition, they continued to manifest higher levels of deviant behaviors during the posttreatment interval and were more likely to meet criteria for antisocial personality disorder.

Collectively, concurrent and prospective studies across a range of adolescent samples (e.g., representative community samples, treatment samples) clearly support an important role for childhood disruptive behaviors as potential precursors of more serious levels of alcohol involvement by adolescents that may well extend into adulthood. Within the adult alcohol-related literature, this early onset pattern of disruptive, antisocial behaviors is linked with the subsequent expression of an adult alcohol disorder that has been identified as an antisocial alcoholic subtype (Cloninger et al., 1981; Zucker & Gomberg, 1986). However, several important questions remain to be addressed about the role of childhood disruptive behaviors and the subsequent expression of alcohol disorders. For example, are there specific disruptive behaviors (e.g., proactive aggression, violence) that are more highly associated with the subsequent expression of alcohol problems during adolescence and alcohol disorders in adulthood than other disruptive behaviors (e.g., oppositional behavior)? There is some evidence, for example, that attentional-deficit—hyperactivity disorder, independent of coexisting conduct disorder, is not significantly related to subsequent problem drinking among adolescents and adults (August et al., 1983; Blouin et al., 1978), though its co-occurrence with conduct disorder may exacerbate the severity of alcohol disorder symptoms.

A second question of importance pertains to the etiology of, and causal relations between, conduct disorder and early-onset problem drinking. Do these two constellations of behaviors share common etiologic origins (e.g., via shared genetic mechanisms, high levels of impulsivity and behavioral undercontrol)? If so, what are the explanatory mechanisms (e.g., early entry to deviant peer networks, deviant self-labeling) that account for this relationship, and why does such a function operate selectively? Not all children manifesting disruptive behaviors or disruptive behavior disorders develop alcohol disorders, and high-end estimates are that only about 25% of alcoholics are antisocial alcoholics. The role of childhood disorders other than disruptive disorders, such anxiety and depressive disorders, have not been as extensively studied in relation to adolescent (or adult) alcohol-related behaviors, even though the adult literature clearly indicates substantial rates of comorbidity among adult alcoholics (Helzer & Pryzbek, 1988; Kessler et al., 1997). This is likely to become a focus in subsequent research on childhood and adolescent psychopathology and substance use.

Alcohol Expectancies

Alcohol expectancies have been consistently associated with earlier onset of alcohol use, higher levels of alcohol use (e.g., frequency and quantity), and prospective transitions to increased levels of alcohol use (Christiansen, Smith, Roehling, & Goldman, 1989; Reese, Chassin, & Molina, 1994; Smith, Goldman, Greenbaum, & Christiansen, 1995). Alcohol expectancies have emerged from social learning theory formulations and are hypothesized to be cognitively based mediators and proximal influences on alcohol-related behaviors (Smith & Goldman, 1994). These expectancies, based on early (and ongoing) learning experiences and anticipated outcomes associated with alcohol use, form memory associations in the form of if-then relations between behavior and its consequences. For example, if someone drinks alcohol, then they are able to think more clearly. As such, according to theory, these alcohol expectancies are important to understand because they may reflect subjective utilities (e.g., cost benefits) associated with alcohol use. Furthermore, to the extent that alcohol expectancies are learned behaviors that are potent mediators and proximal causes of alcohol use, they may serve as highly suitable targets for modification with cognitive-behavioral-based interventions.

Much of the initial research on alcohol expectancies was conducted with adults, but there have been an ongoing and expanding number of studies with adolescents. Christiansen, Goldman, and Inn (1982) provided support that adolescents were capable of differentiating alcohol expectancies in a manner similar to adults. The adolescents in their study identified several different moderately to highly correlated alcohol expectancies that referred to beliefs that using alcohol was a powerful agent that can make global, positive transformations of experience, can enhance or impede social behaviors, improve cognitive performance, enhance sexuality, increase arousal, and promote relaxation. Cross-sectional studies of the interrelationships between alcohol expectancies and adolescent alcohol use have consistently demonstrated high, positive associations (Mann, Chassin, & Sher, 1987). In a prospective study, Christiansen et al. (1989) reported that alcohol expectancies held by nondrinking seventh and eighth graders (students who had consumed four or fewer drinks in their lifetime) predicted over 25% of the variance in level of alcohol use 12 months later. In addition, five of the seven alcohol expectancy scales assessed at the first occasion of measurement differed significantly between those adolescents who became problem drinkers at the second occasion of measurement (after a 1-year interval) and those adolescents who were not problem drinkers at the second occasion.

Three other prospective studies have also supported the utility of adolescent alcohol expectancies as short-term and long-term predictors of alcohol-related behaviors. Prospective, bidirectional relationships between alcohol use and alcohol expectancies were supported with two independent adolescent samples (Bauman, Fisher, Bryan, & Chenowith, 1985; Smith et al., 1995). That is, alcohol use prospectively predicted alcohol expectancies and alcohol expectancies prospectively predicted alcohol use. The findings of Stacy, Newcomb, and Bentler (1992) indicated that adolescent expectancies predicted substance use 9 years later, after controlling statistically for initial levels of adolescent substance use. Reese et al. (1994) used a two-wave research design (with a 1-year interval between occasions of measurement) with a sample of early adolescents (mean age = 12.78 years) to investigate the influence of Occasion 1 alcohol expectancies on Occasion 2 alcohol problems (e.g., complaints from family or friends about adolescent's drinking, trying to cut down but not able to) while controlling for Occasion 1 alcohol consumption and the status of family history of alcoholism. The findings indicated that alcohol expectancies were statistically significant prospective predictors of alcohol problems, albeit at low levels of magnitude (e.g., accounting for 2%-3% of additional variance in Occasion 2 outcome variables).

In addition to these more survey-based empirical findings supporting the predictive utility of alcohol expectancies, Deckel, Hesselbrock, and Bauer (1995) have provided some initial data on associations between alcohol expectancies and peripheral electrophysiological and neuropsychological measures of brain functioning. Specifically, with a nonclinical sample of young adult males (n = 91), Deckel et al. regressed selected frontal and parietal electroencephalogram (EEG) power spectra measures and neuropsychological measures of prefrontal-frontal brain functioning (e.g., perseverative errors from the Wisconsin Card Sort test, Porteus Maze Test) on alcohol expectancies via the multiple regression statistical model. Regression analyses indicated that the selected neuropsychological tests accounted for 17.5% of the variance for a scale assessing Global Alcohol Expectancies, 16% of the variance for a scale assessing Alcohol Sexual Enhancement Expectancies, and 9% of the variance for a scale measuring Alcohol Social Expectancies. The findings from the EEG power spectra measures supported statistically significant relationships for the frontal but not the parietal locations, with variance accounted for ranging from 5% to 12% for the alcohol expectancy scale scores.

Deckel et al. (1995) interpreted these findings as providing support that alcohol expectancies may be partially biologically determined via individual differences in the frontal-prefrontal systems of the brain and mediated neurochemically by brain serotonin levels. Furthermore, Deckel et al. proposed that such biologically influenced expectancies have the potential to be premorbid risk factors identifiable in childhood or adolescence and as such may serve as early markers for targeted alcohol interventions. The findings of Deckel et al. are best viewed cautiously and in need of replication, but they do offer the prospect of important integrations across levels of analysis (e.g., biological, cognitive, social), with implications for prevention research.

Level of Religiosity

Level of religiosity has often been identified as a protective factor for the early onset of and progression toward serious involvement with alcohol among adolescents (Bahr, Hawks, & Wang, 1993; Kandel, 1980). A low, negative correlation between level of religious commitment and alcohol use has been the prototypical empirical finding, though there has been some variability in the strength of the association contingent on the manner in which religiosity was measured. Three aspects of religious involvement that are often measured in studies of adolescents are *affiliation, attendance,* and *beliefs.* All three may be important, contingent on the specific nature of the research question, but these three need not manifest a pattern of high covariation (or correlation) with each other. For instance, frequent church attendance may result from parental demands that do not correspond with strongly held religious beliefs by adolescents; conversely, strong religious beliefs may exist quite independent of frequency of church attendance or affiliation. Part of the inconsistency in the magnitude of the association between religiosity and adolescent alcohol use arises from variability in which aspect of religiosity is assessed.

Critical analyses of the negative association between level of religiosity and alcohol use have indicated that the low magnitude association commonly reported at the bivariate level (Pearson r) is attenuated and frequently not statistically significant when other variables are included in multiple-predictor models. For example, after including the variables of parental monitoring and family drug use, Bahr et al. (1993) reported that religious importance was not significantly associated with peer drug use or current adolescent substance use. Thus, level of religiosity, in and of itself, may not be a consistent, potent predictor of adolescent alcohol use. However, the inadequate conceptualization and measurement of level of religiosity precludes a definitive statement about the potential value of this concept and its relation to adolescent alcohol use. Furthermore, level of religiosity may be more optimally conceptualized as an indirect effect (influenced by and influencing family relationships and community ties) rather than as a direct effect, or conceptualized within a more "nested" social-ecological framework, where church or religious affiliation may serve as higher-order units of analysis. The latter application may involve the use of hierarchical, or multilevel, models to evaluate individual variation in adolescent alcohol use within and between second-order units, such as churches that may vary in their level of tolerance of alcohol (for more on multilevel models, see Bryk & Raudenbush, 1992; Goldstein, 1995).

Age of Onset for Alcohol Use

In some research applications, age of onset for alcohol use has been used as a dependent variable, and other variables (e.g., poor parental monitoring, deviant peer affiliations) have been used as predictor variables (Webb, Baer, McLaughlin, McKelvy, & Caid, 1991). In other research applications, age of onset has been used as a marker, or predictor, variable for heavier drinking in adolescence or for the prediction of an alcohol or psychiatric disorder in adulthood (Barnes & Welte, 1986; Buydens-Branchey, Branchey, Noumair, & Lieber, 1989). With regard to the latter research on age of onset, different indicators of early onset have been associated with poorer adolescent and adult outcomes. With a sample of over 27,000 students in grades 7 through 12 in New York State, Barnes and Welte (1986) reported that age of first intoxication significantly predicted level of current alcohol use; those students who reported getting intoxicated by age 11 years or younger reported drinking an average of almost four drinks a day, whereas those students who reported never getting intoxicated reported drinking an average of less than one drink a month. Yu and Williford (1992) examined the age of alcohol use onset in relation to subsequent drug use activity with a representative sample of young adults (aged 16-24 years) in New York State. Their findings indicated that alcohol use onset, especially between the ages of 13 and 16, was important in predicting current alcohol and marijuana use; hence, these findings suggest a critical age interval (13-16 years of age) for alcohol onset to affect subsequent substance use.

With a nationally representative sample of adults retrospectively reporting on their age of onset for alcohol use, the younger the age of onset, the greater the probability that a person would develop an alcohol disorder in their lifetime (Grant & Dawson, 1998). Those adults who reported initiating alcohol use before age 15 years were 4 times more likely to develop alcohol dependence than those who delayed initiation until age 21 years. In a study of alcoholic patients in treatment, Buydens-Branchey et al. (1989) found that the onset of an alcohol disorder prior to age 20 years was associated with a higher incidence of paternal alcoholism. Furthermore, this earlier-onset group, relative to the later-onset group (onset of alcohol disorder past age 20), was twice as likely to have been incarcerated for crimes related to physical violence, was 3 times as likely to be depressed, and 4 times as likely to have attempted suicide.

These findings suggest that an earlier onset of alcohol use, alcohol intoxication, or alcohol disorder is prognostic of subsequent problems in areas related to alcohol abuse and psychiatric disturbance. The concept of a critical period for alcohol use onset has not been firmly established, though the emerging evidence is clear in suggesting that prevention efforts that target delays in the onset of alcohol use are largely supported by the literature. Yet much remains to be known as to whether there is something intrinsic and fundamentally causal about earlier alcohol onset or whether it is a proxy or marker variable for a constellation of other dysfunctional processes (e.g., family dysfunction, genetic diathesis).

General Coping Strategies and
Alcohol-Specific Drinking Motives

Lazarus and Folkman (1984) described two major coping styles in response to stressors. *Problem-focused* coping corresponded with behavioral efforts to directly and constructively alter the source of the stressor, and *emotion-focused* coping corresponded with cognitive efforts to mitigate the distress associated with the stressor. Correlational analyses with adolescent samples have indicated that problem-focused coping is inversely related to alcohol use and to alcohol problems (Windle & Windle, 1996). That is, adolescents who typically respond directly to stressors with planful, task-oriented strategies to resolve the necessary stressor-related issues consume less alcohol and have fewer alcohol problems. In the Windle and Windle study, emotion-focused coping was positively correlated with alcohol problems but not significantly associated with alcohol use. Thus, those adolescents who tended to ruminate more and to engage in self-blame were more likely to have more alcohol problems. These findings were consistent with those reported by Myers and Brown (1990) in their study of coping and relapse among 50 adolescents treated for alcohol and drug abuse. Those adolescents with the poorest relapse outcomes generated the fewest coping strategies to a hypothetical, high-risk relapse situation. Moreover, they used fewer problem-solving coping strategies and had lower self-efficacy in high-risk relapse situations in general.

A third coping style that has arisen in the literature is *avoidance* coping, and it corresponds to activities that either deny the existence of, or postpone addressing, the stressor. Positive associations have been reported between avoidance coping and alcohol problems, but a nonsignificant relationship was indicated for avoidance coping and alcohol use (Windle & Windle, 1996). This positive association between avoidance coping and alcohol problems differs from the inverse relationship reported by others in the literature (Cooper, Russell, & George, 1988), but this is because avoidance coping has been defined in alternative ways. Cooper et al. defined avoidance coping as the engagement in behaviors that may be viewed as unhealthy (e.g., increased eating or smoking, social isolation), whereas the measure used by Windle and Windle defined avoidance coping as engagement in pleasantly distracting activities (e.g., watching TV, phoning a friend). The prosocial nature of the latter definition of avoidance coping may reflect a more firmly entrenched relationship with peer networks (possibly deviant peer networks) that contributed to the positive association between avoidance coping and alcohol problems among adolescents. It is important in subsequent research on adolescent coping and substance use to include both negative and positive features of avoidance coping and to analyze contextual conditions (e.g., extensiveness and level of deviance of peer group) that may moderate associations or influence the direction and magnitude of effects or both.

In addition to the limited literature on general coping strategies and adolescent alcohol-related behaviors, there have been a number of studies that have examined associations between adolescent alcohol use and motives for drinking. Motives for alcohol use refer to the self-ascribed reasons for using alcohol. They differ from general coping strategies in that they are specific to reasons for using alcohol; they are different from alcohol expectancies in that they refer to motivations for drinking (e.g., to escape the stressors of daily living) and not necessarily what one expects from the use of alcohol (e.g., to increase social or cognitive functioning). Hence, one may expect alcohol to increase sexual arousal, but one may be motivated to drink to escape from perceived daily pressures.

Much of the limited research on motives for drinking among adolescents has focused on two motive categories: *Coping motives* refer to drinking to avoid adverse (or negatively stressful) conditions, and *social motives* refer to drinking to socialize with others and to celebrate special occasions with friends. More frequent use of coping motives for drinking have been consistently associated with higher levels of alcohol use and alcohol problems (Cooper, 1994; Windle & Windle, 1996). In the Windle and Windle study, coping motives for drinking significantly predicted not only alcohol-related outcomes but also depressed affect and delinquency, after controlling for general coping strategies, family social support, and three domains of life events (major, positive daily, and negative daily events). Further research is merited on coping motives for drinking and the generalizability of this characteristic to other domains of behavior (for an emotion-regulatory model incorporating this notion, see Labouvie, 1986). Social motives for drinking have also been significantly associated with adolescent alcohol use, albeit at a lower magnitude than coping motives, but such motives have not been consistently associated with alcohol problems or problem drinking (Cooper, 1994; Windle & Barnes, 1988; Windle & Windle, 1996).

Cooper (1994) identified two additional adolescent drinking motives that have sporadically appeared in the literature. *Social conformity* motives refer to drinking so as not to be rejected by your peer group and to feel like you are part of the crowd. Statistically significant correlations were reported between conformity motives and alcohol use but not problem drinking. Cooper proposed that conformity motives may be more highly associated with early experimentation with alcohol, prior to the establishment of more internalized beliefs about the substance or more established and regulated patterns of peer group selection, socialization, and drinking behaviors. *Enhancement* motives refer to drinking so as to increase positive affect (e.g., pleasurable, euphoric emotional states). Cooper, as well as Windle and Barnes (1988), reported that enhancement motives predicted both alcohol use and heavy drinking. Although additional research is needed on all motives for drinking, enhancement-motivated drinking may be an especially important attribute because it may signal potential problems as an early indicator of increased tolerance or of a need or desire to ingest a variety of other drugs to increase positive affective states; increasingly higher levels of use across time may culminate in undesirable end states (an alcohol or other substance abuse disorder).

PEER INFLUENCES

Perhaps the most frequently cited influence on adolescent alcohol use in the popular press is that of peers. In fact, many early (and extant) prevention programs have been based on the premise that peer pressure is the primary social culprit for adolescents engaging in alcohol use. The empirical literature has consistently supported the importance of peers in accounting for adolescent alcohol use (Chassin, Pillow, Curran, Molina & Barrera, 1993; Kandel, 1980; Oetting & Beauvais, 1986) but not necessarily through peer pressure mechanisms, which imply some sort of overt or covert coercive process, whereby totally unwitting adolescents are suddenly and unwillingly consuming alcoholic beverages. Rather, peer influences appear to operate via both initial selection processes and subsequent reciprocal socialization processes. Reed and Rountree (1997) provided support for peer selection and socialization influences on adolescent substance use, in addition to cognitive shifts toward more (shared) favorable attitudes toward use; overt peer pressure was not a significant influence. Hence, peer selection is not a random process but rather involves more sophisticated social interactional patterns of selection, deselection and dropping out of one peer group, and establishing affiliations with new peer groups, based on common interests and activities. Such interests and activities may be focused on musical interests or scholastic events or on deviant activities, including alcohol use. As escalatory cycles are initiated into heavier alcohol use or drug use, some members drop out of peer groups, whereas others increase the peer bond associated with given activities.

In many of the prediction studies of peer influences on adolescent alcohol use, the number or percentage of alcohol-using friends is the most potent predictor of adolescent alcohol use, sometimes accounting for as much as 50% of the variance (Chassin et al., 1993; Wills et al., 1998). These findings are important and do indeed highlight the significance of the peer context to adolescent drinking. However, there are two important elements that such predictor studies do not accomplish. First, many of these studies are cross-sectional, and hence there is no way of disentangling peer selection versus peer socialization effects. Second and more important, the operationalization of the peer variables assessed (e.g., number of alcohol-using peers) functions more as a proxy variable for group affiliation and does not provide insight into the underlying causal processes that would facilitate a more comprehensive understanding of the specific processes underlying peer selection, reciprocal socialization, and alcohol use. This knowledge could prove invaluable to prevention studies that attempt to target the peer group itself or peer group influences.

Windle (1994) focused on relational features of adolescents with their best friends and reported that higher levels of adolescent alcohol use were associated with best friendships rated as higher in overt and covert conflict and lower in reciprocity of relations. Therefore, whether such variation in best-friendship qualities is due to selection or socialization influences is not known, but the nature of best friendships among heavier drinkers did differ significantly from the best-friendship relations among lighter drinkers. More knowledge about such sources of variation in friendships according to level of adolescent alcohol involvement, their origins via selection processes, and their time course via reciprocal socialization processes may facilitate a greater understanding of the processes whereby peer influences have their effects.

FAMILY INFLUENCES

Family influences have been prominent correlates and predictors of adolescent alcohol use. The source of these family influences (genetic or environmental) is still subject to occasional debate, but the emerging consensus is that both are important and that the relative influences may vary, contingent on the phenotype studied (e.g., severe alcohol dependence vs. frequency of alcohol use) and the age period in the lifespan under investigation (Heath, 1995; McGue, 1994). This section focuses on presumed socialization influences rather than direct genetic contributions (for genetic contributions, see the earlier discussion on family history of alcoholism).

Social learning theory formulations and derivative minitheories of alcohol use have hypothesized that role modeling and imitation are learning processes that account for significant associations regarding resemblance between parental and offspring drinking patterns. The research findings have been fairly consistent in supporting a significant association, albeit of low to moderate magnitude, between levels of maternal and paternal alcohol use and adolescent offspring use (Barnes, 1990; Hops, Tildesley, Lichtenstein, Ary, & Sherman, 1990; Webb & Baer, 1995). Thompson and Wilsnack (1987) reported statistically significant correlations between early adolescents' (seventh and eighth graders) perceptions of parental alcohol use and the self-reported use of alcohol by these adolescents 4 years later. Note that the studies referred are based on nonclinical samples of families and need to be distinguished from studies of selected subpopulations, such as children of alcoholics, where intergenerational associations for alcohol use are often much stronger.

In addition to role modeling and imitative influences by parents, considerable research interest has focused on the role of parenting practices and family interactional processes that may contribute to adolescent alcohol use (for reviews, see Barnes, 1990; Jacob & Leonard, 1994). With regard to parenting practices, four domains have been identified as significantly associated with adolescent alcohol use. *Parental nurturance,* or level of emotional warmth and support, has been consistently inversely related with level of adolescent alcohol use (Barnes, 1990). Those parents who are viewed by their adolescents as more caring, concerned, and supportive of them have offspring who initiate alcohol use later and consume lower levels of alcohol. Higher levels of *parental monitoring,* or establishing and enforcing reasonable rules for adolescent conduct, have also been inversely related to adolescent alcohol use. That is, the adolescents of parents who establish explicit rules and boundary conditions for permissible adolescent behaviors (regarding curfew, hours of study per day) and reasonable, consistently enforced contingencies for rule violations tend to initiate alcohol use later and to consume alcohol less frequently. Higher levels of *time spent together* by adolescents and their parents is associated with lower levels of adolescent alcohol use, as is higher levels of *parent-adolescent communication.* Although all of these parenting behaviors may be distinguished conceptually and methodologically, at a higher level, they all may reflect common processes related to level of parental involvement or investment in their adolescent offspring, with higher parental involvement associated with a greater internalization by the adolescents of parental norms for drinking. Furthermore, the more leisure time that parents spend with their adolescent offspring may decrease the amount of time spent with peers and indirectly influence peer selection processes that are important in understanding adolescent alcohol use. A number of family variables have also been associated with levels of adolescent alcohol use. For example, higher levels of marital conflict and marital dissatisfaction have been associated with more adolescent alcohol use (Seilhamer & Jacob, 1990). Similarly, higher levels of stressful family events and violence within the family have been associated with earlier onset and more involved patterns of alcohol use by adolescents. In families with an alcoholic parent, there is a range of familial and parenting processes that contribute to heightened inconsistency in parenting practices, greater spousal and child abuse, greater spousal conflict, and more stressful events (financial strain associated with sporadic employment by alcoholic parent) that may undermine a relatively stable, emotionally supportive context for adolescent development (for reviews, see Seilhamer & Jacob, 1990; Windle & Tubman, in press). This instability may contribute to earlier and more severe patterns of alcohol involvement by adolescents who seek to escape from the unpleasantries of the home environment as they move more rapidly, and perhaps prematurely, toward a more deviant peer context for social and emotional support.

In addition to parental influences on adolescent drinking, older siblings have also been identified as role models and influential agents that contribute to higher rates of adolescent alcohol use (Ary, Tildesley, Hops, & Andrews, 1993; Needle, McCubbin, Reineck, Lazar, & Mederer, 1986). With an adolescent sample ranging in age from 11 to 17 years, Ary et al. (1993) reported a concurrent (i.e., cross-sectional) regression coefficient of .44 ($p < .001$) between older sibling alcohol use and younger adolescent alcohol use. On the basis of a sample of 508 families with a focal adolescent aged 11 to 13 years and an older sibling aged 14 to 18 years, the findings of Needle et al. (1986) indicated statistically significant associations between older sibling and younger sibling alcohol use. Specifically, if older siblings were nonusers of alcohol in the past year, more than 90% of the focal adolescents reported nonuse in the past year. If older siblings reported using alcohol 20 or more times in the past year, more than 25% of the younger, focal adolescents reported usage.

In a quite intriguing adoptee study by McGue, Sharma, and Benson (1996), relatively substantial sibling environmental effects were cited. The sample consisted of 653 adoptive families selected from adoption agencies in four U.S. states, including 255 pairs of non-biologically-related siblings. The use of pairs of non-biologically-related siblings is very useful because the correlation between such siblings provides a direct estimate of the percentage of variance in the phenotype (e.g., alcohol use) associated with the siblings' common rearing (Plomin, DeFries, & McClearn, 1990). The derived correlation assumes that there is no selective placement of adoptees into families; violations of this assumption will inflate the adoptee-sibling correlation. McGue et al. (1996) reported an adoptee-sibling correlation for level of alcohol involvement (defined by a composite measure of frequency of use, binge drinking, and alcohol problems) as $r = .239$ ($p < .01$); therefore, approximately 24% of the variance associated with alcohol involvement was attributable to common rearing effects.

Additional analyses were conducted with the nonbiological siblings by categorizing them according to a few demographic characteristics. The adoptee-sibling correlation was greater for pairs who were similar or near in age ($r = .349$) than for those dissimilar or distant in age ($r = .047$), and same-sex correlations ($r = .356$) were larger than opposite-sex correlations ($r = .182$), though these latter correlations did not differ at the conventional alpha level of $p < .05$ but rather at $p < .07$. Same ($r = .205$) versus different ($r = .396$) ethnicity among the adoptee-sibling pairs did not reveal a statistically significant difference ($p < .10$), but limited statistical power restricted a more powerful test of statistical differences in the magnitude of these correlations. The findings by McGue et al. (1996) clearly support the notion of substantial common rearing (environmental) effects for siblings, with a variable magnitude of association contingent on demographic characteristics (e.g., gender, age differences). They further reported in their study that parental problem drinking and family functioning were not strongly associated with adolescent alcohol use, hence the common rearing effects were more likely attributable to sibling influences (e.g., older siblings influencing younger siblings via role modeling or providing access) or to other common rearing influences (e.g., common peers).

The findings by McGue et al. (1996) highlight another important issue found in the literature regarding the relative roles of parent and sibling influences on adolescent alcohol use. Most studies of family influences on adolescent alcohol use have not included siblings as potential influential agents. This has precluded the investigation of an important, albeit understudied, research question pertinent to the combined influences of parents, siblings, and peers. Such research questions are important because they provide a larger frame of reference for understanding the multiplicity of influences and potential synergistic (interactive) relationships that account for variation in adolescent alcohol use. For example, Needle et al. (1986) reported a statistically significant interaction between older sibling and peer hard liquor use and target adolescent hard liquor use; the synergistic interaction indicated that hard liquor use by the younger adolescent was substantially stronger when both older siblings and peers consumed hard liquor than when only one or the other consumed hard liquor. Such potential synergistic relations have infrequently been studied in the family-peer research conducted to date. Such inquiries into synergistic relations may increase our understanding of the complexities and multipredictor mediator and moderator relationships that more adequately characterize the multiple social influences on adolescent alcohol use.

There have been a large number of studies examining parent-adolescent resemblance for drinking and a rapidly increasing number that include measures of peer alcohol use; fewer have also included siblings, though the trend is changing toward including measures of sibling drinking or including siblings as part of a larger family research design. The generalization that appears to have emerged based on the extant literature (Ary et al., 1993; Needle et al., 1986) is that, with regard to adolescent alcohol use, peer influences are the most potent, sibling influences are the second most potent, and parental influences are the least potent. This ordering may vary somewhat, contingent on the age of the adolescent (parental monitoring influences may be somewhat stronger with younger adolescents) and the phenotype studied (e.g., parental influences may be more important for alcohol use onset than frequency or quantity of use), but the generalization holds across this first generation of descriptive association studies. More refined research questions and associated sophisticated methodologies (e.g., prospective research designs, multimethod assessments, social network analyses, more precise measures of peer and sibling relationships) are needed to more fully comprehend the nature of these interrelated parent, sibling, and peer influences on adolescent alcohol use. Furthermore, such investigations need to study the multiple phenotypes associated with alcohol behaviors (e.g., onset, heavy use, alcohol problems, dependency symptoms, the expression of an alcohol disorder) because there may be common and unique parental, sibling, and peer influences for these phenotypes.

SOCIETAL AND COMMUNITY-LEVEL FACTORS

There are a number of societal, community, and cultural factors that foster or inhibit alcohol use behaviors by adolescents. For example, some U.S. state counties are "wet" (sell alcohol) and others are "dry" (do not sell alcohol), thus potentially influencing both exposure to and ease of access to alcohol.

Similarly, the densities of alcohol outlets in communities influence normative standards of drinking and frequency of alcohol-related problems, such as drinking and violence or drinking and driving crashes and fatalities (Gruenewald et al., 1996).

There are numerous culture-related differences across racial and ethnic groups that contribute to variability in the drinking practices of adolescents (Bettes, Dusenbury, Kerner, James-Ortiz, & Botvin, 1990; Maddahian, Newcomb, & Bentler, 1988; Rhodes, Gingiss, & Smith, 1994). The limited number of cross-national (or international) studies have also identified significant variability in drinking practices among youth (Adler & Kandel, 1983; Christiansen & Teahan, 1987). For instance, Christiansen and Teahan reported that Irish, relative to U.S., adolescents reported less social and problematic drinking and had lower alcohol expectancies for improved cognitive and motor functioning; however, they had higher expectancies for increased aggression while drinking. The origins and consequences of cultural differences in adolescent drinking await further study and will provide a useful laboratory for studying societal influences.

Although there have been a limited number of international (or cross-cultural) studies of adolescent drinking, there is an evolving literature focused on social influences on adolescent drinking practices and their consequences. Such coverage is beyond the scope of this book. However, an important and telling illustration of societal influences on adolescent drinking in the United States is that of access and legal enforcement of drinking among adolescents. It is illegal for a minor (under age 21) to purchase or consume alcohol and illegal for an adult to sell alcohol to or buy alcohol for a minor. Nevertheless, it is widely recognized that adolescents can easily access alcohol, do so frequently, and consume large quantities with a fair degree of regularity (Johnston et al., 1996). Research indicates that adolescents obtain alcoholic beverages either directly through a regular commercial outlet (bar, liquor store) or from an adult (friend, sibling) who is of legal age (Wagenaar et al., 1993). In an interesting study of the "success" of the underage purchasing of alcohol, Wagenaar and Wolfson (1995) had "young looking" 21-year-old women attempt to purchase liquor in 910 alcohol outlets across the upper Midwest in Minnesota and Wisconsin. Of these, 47% of off-sale sites (e.g., take-out outlets, convenience stores) and 46% of on-sale outlets (e.g., bars and taverns) sold liquor to these buyers without requesting age identification. Furthermore, when the women who were sold the liquor without a request for age identification then requested a receipt for the sale, the sales clerks were resistant to providing one. The sales clerks feared potential identification, should a legal suit somehow arise (e.g., a drinking-driving crash) from the sale of alcohol to minors. Hence, it appeared that these sales clerks had suspicions about the age of the buyers but did not request age identification. These findings regarding the lack of enforcement of underage drinking laws are consistent with other studies. Wolfson, Wagenaar, and Hornseth (1995) conducted in-depth interviews with police officers in four states who reported that there was high community tolerance and acceptance of youthful drinking and that few police resources were directed toward this issue. Furthermore, there was wide variability across police officers as to what exactly was illegal with regard to adolescent alcohol (e.g., possession, consumption, its purchase) and what the appropriate sequential process was when encountering an adolescent who had been drinking. Wagenaar and Wolfson (1994) also reported on a four-state study of arrests for underage drinking across a 3-year period (1988 to 1990). In 12% of the counties of these four states, there were no arrests for underage drinking, 25% of the counties had no actions against alcohol outlets for sales to minors, and 41% of the counties reported no arrests for adults purchasing alcohol for minors.

In sum, there appears to be very little societal support in the United States for the enforcement of laws surrounding underage drinking by adolescents. This lax view toward adolescent alcohol use contrasts quite sharply with that toward other illicit substances (e.g., marijuana, cocaine). Hence, at the societal level, the failure to enforce laws pertinent to adolescent drinking does little to constrain access to alcoholic beverages by adolescents.

SUMMARY

This chapter has provided a description of a range of risk and protective factors associated with adolescent alcohol use. The identified factors span levels of analysis from the molecular to the social-cultural. Whereas scientific evidence has been provided for each of these factors, the current research agenda has branched in two related directions. First, there is much research that is focusing on mediator and moderator models to more adequately evaluate the influence of one or more risk or protective factors (or both) on adolescent substance use (Chassin et al., 1993; Sher, 1991). An objective of this research is to more adequately understand the mechanisms or processes that account for the presumed putative influences of the risk and protective factors. Second, there have been efforts to combine, or pool, multiple risk and multiple protective factors in the same model to examine the simultaneous predictive relations of the multitude of variables that have been identified in the literature (Jessor, Van Den Bos, Vanderryn, Costa, & Turbin, 1995; Newcomb & Felix-Ortiz, 1992). Both of these research agendas are likely to continue to be of importance to the research literature for a number of years ahead, as efforts continue to understand individual variation in intraindividual (within person) trajectories associated with alcohol use from childhood through adulthood.

4

APPROACHES TO THE PREVENTION
OF ALCOHOL USE AND ABUSE

Prevention approaches to adolescent alcohol use have expanded considerably in recent years. Much of the early prevention research in the 1970s and early-to-mid-1980s focused almost exclusively on educationally based school prevention programs. Recent prevention efforts have broadened the intervention targets to include individual, family, school, and community (e.g., police, media sources, server providers), as well as the implementation and evaluation of social policies (e.g., minimum drinking age laws) on specific health-related outcomes (e.g., teenage alcohol-related automobile crashes or fatalities). Conceptual models of preventive interventions are often categorized into three types—primary, secondary, and tertiary. *Primary* interventions focus on populations not necessarily currently experiencing a problem but who are, collectively, at risk due to age-normative trends in drinking. *Secondary* interventions focus on populations that are manifesting some level of problematic behaviors (e.g., currently drinking alcohol), and efforts are made to prevent the escalation of these behaviors to more serious levels or to more serious consequences. *Tertiary* interventions focus on populations that are (or have) experienced serious consequences associated with their behavior (alcohol-related legal encounters, missing school due to drinking). As such, the primary, secondary, and tertiary approaches provide for a continuum of interventions contingent on the level or severity of the problem.

SUBSTANCE USE
PREVENTIVE INTERVENTIONS

In this section, I review several different types of adolescent substance use prevention programs, including universal, school-based programs; targeted programs for adolescents at risk for developing substance-related problems; family-based programs; and comprehensive community-wide programs. Many of these programs include a focus on the prevention of both alcohol use and other substance use (e.g., cigarettes, illicit drugs) among adolescents. The term *substance use intervention* is used in this chapter to refer to interventions that include a focus on alcohol *and* other substances; alcohol-specific interventions will be so designated. Research findings relevant to alcohol use are emphasized, but findings relevant to other substance use are also reported when deemed important to appreciate the goals and efficacy of the intervention. My purpose in this chapter is not to provide a comprehensive review of the adolescent alcohol prevention literature (for recent reviews, see Gorman, 1995, 1996a; Gorman & Speer, 1996) but rather to present a description of the rationale, program design, and empirical findings from several highly visible preventive interventions.

A central goal common to the preventive interventions discussed is their focus on intervening for the purpose of affecting positive changes in the underlying causes of adolescent substance use initiation and continuation. The targets of change vary and are dependent on the conceptual models on which the interventions are based. For example, many universal, school-based substance use prevention programs are based on a social-influence model, which suggests that the primary influences affecting youths' substance use behaviors are social factors, such as peer, family, and media influences. As such, these programs are aimed at helping adolescents to acquire skills that will enable them to effectively resist social pressures (especially peer pressures) to use substances and at changing social attitudes and norms in an anti-substance-use direction (Bauman & Ennett, 1996; Gorman, 1995, 1996a; Norman & Turner, 1993). In contrast, comprehensive community-wide preventive interventions, such as Project Northland (Perry et al., 1996), view the causes of adolescent substance use from a multivariate, multilevel perspective and thus target intrapersonal, interpersonal, social, and policy variables for change. Such programs focus on decreasing both adolescents' demand for and their access (or supply) to tobacco, alcohol, and other substances (Williams, Perry, Farbakhsh, & Veblen-Mortenson, in press).

Universal, School-Based Preventive Interventions

During the decade of the 1980s, the most popular form of adolescent substance use prevention programs was universal, school-based curricula that used a social-influence model (also referred to as a *social environmental model*) for program development (Gorman, 1996b; Norman & Turner, 1993).

A primary assumption of the social-influence model is that adolescent substance use occurs as a consequence of important social influences (e.g., peers and the media) that exert pressure on adolescents to use tobacco, alcohol, and other substances; as such, a crucial goal of programs based on this model is to teach adolescents the requisite skills that will help them to resist social pressures to use substances (Norman & Turner, 1993). Two of the most popular types of school-based programs—resistance skills training and social-skills training—are predicated on a social-influence approach (Gorman, 1995, 1996a). The focus of social-skills training programs is broader than that of resistance skills training programs, in that the former acknowledges a number of psychological (e.g., cognitions, attitudes, expectations) and social risk factors as contributing to adolescent substance use, whereas the latter is concerned primarily with social pressures (especially peer pressure) to use drugs. As a consequence, social-skills training programs assist adolescents to acquire both general and specific skills, such as communication and coping skills and alcohol refusal skills, that will enhance their development of competencies to resist substance use behaviors. In contrast, resistance skills training programs are concerned primarily with helping teens to identify social pressures to use substances and to acquire the skills needed to resist such pressures (Norman & Turner, 1993).

The efficacy of three universal, school-based substance use prevention programs based on a social-influence framework is reviewed in the following discussion, along with findings from long-term follow-up studies. These programs are Project ALERT (Ellickson & Bell, 1990; Ellickson, Bell, & McGuigan, 1993), Life Skills Training (LST; Botvin, Baker, Dusenbury, Botvin, & Diaz, 1995; Botvin, Baker, Dusenbury, Tortu, & Botvin, 1990), and the Alcohol Misuse Prevention Study (AMPS; Dielman, Shope, Butchart, & Campanelli, 1986; Dielman, Shope, Leech, & Butchart, 1989; Shope, Dielman, Butchart, Campanelli, & Kloska, 1992).

Project ALERT (Ellickson & Bell, 1990; Ellickson et al., 1993) is a universal, school-based, resistance skills training program based on a social-influence model. A primary focus of the program is on teaching young adolescents the skills and strategies they need to resist both internal and external pressures to use tobacco, alcohol, and marijuana. Project ALERT involved 30 junior high schools in California and Oregon that were randomly assigned to three treatment conditions. Ten schools were assigned to a control condition in which they did not receive the Project ALERT curriculum, but they continued any substance use prevention programs they were currently implementing. Ten schools were assigned to a Project ALERT treatment condition in which adult health educators presented the intervention curriculum, and ten schools were assigned to a Project ALERT condition in which both adult health educators and older teen leaders administered the curriculum. The study participants were heterogeneous in terms of racial background, SES, and family composition.

The Project ALERT curriculum was taught to seventh grade students across an 8-week period, with one lesson presented per week. During eighth grade, students received three booster lessons. Self-report questionnaire data on adolescent substance use behaviors were collected at pretest and initial posttest (a 3-month follow-up) during seventh grade and before and after the booster sessions in eighth grade (12-month and 15-month follow-ups). To evaluate Project ALERT's effectiveness at deterring cigarette, alcohol, and marijuana use behaviors among adolescents at different levels of risk, participants were divided into three groups reflecting lesser and greater risk status in relation to these substances. Based on their pretest substance use data, participants were categorized as *nonusers, experimenters,* and *users* for alcohol and cigarettes. Similar procedures were used for marijuana use, and participants were assigned to the following groups: marijuana and cigarette nonusers; marijuana nonusers, cigarette users; and marijuana users. The program effects of Project ALERT were then evaluated by comparing the 3-month, 12-month, and 15-month substance use outcome variables for the three experimental conditions and for the risk groups.

The findings suggested that the program effects on outcome variables across the three time periods (3-month, 12-month, and 15-month follow-up), the three levels of risk status (nonusers, experimenters, and users), and the three experimental conditions (adult health educators, adult health educators plus older teen leaders, and control conditions) were mixed. Several general findings were noteworthy. First, Project ALERT had very few effects on adolescent alcohol use across the 2-year study period. Second, Project ALERT was effective at reducing the use of cigarettes among baseline experimenters in the treatment conditions at the 15-month follow-up; however, it *increased* cigarette use at the 12-month and 15-month follow-ups among baseline users who were in the health educator plus teen leader condition. Third, Project ALERT was effective at reducing the initiation of marijuana use among baseline marijuana and cigarette nonusers in the treatment conditions at the 12-month and 15-month follow-ups.

In a follow-up study evaluating Project ALERT's long-term effectiveness (Ellickson et al., 1993), study participants completed self-report data on their cigarette, alcohol, and marijuana use behaviors in 9th, 10th, and 12th grades (at 24, 36, and 60 months after pretest). In the follow-up study, the three experimental groups were compared on their substance use during grades 10 and 12. Between 53% to 57% of the original study participants (those who participated at the baseline assessment) were included in the 10th-grade and 12th-grade analyses. As with the previous study, students were divided into risk groups based on their pretest use of substances (i.e., nonusers, experimenters, users).

Results from both the 10th-grade and 12th-grade analyses indicated no significant differences among the three experimental groups on their use of cigarettes, alcohol, and marijuana. In general, the positive program effects evident at the 12-month and 15-month follow-ups had disappeared by the 24-month (9th grade) follow-up. Based on these results, Ellickson et al. (1993) concluded that the discontinuation of the Project ALERT curriculum after the 8th grade booster sessions, in combination with adolescents' transition into high-school settings where there are increased pressures to use substances, resulted in the decay of earlier positive program effects. According to the authors, the implication is that substance prevention programs need to be continued into the high-school years.

Botvin et al. (1990) conceptualized the initiation of adolescent substance use as resulting from the interaction of social (e.g., peers, family, and media) and intrapersonal (e.g., cognitions, attitudes, personality) influences. The LST program (Botvin et al., 1990; Botvin et al., 1995) is based on social-influence and cognitive-behavior models and is premised on the idea that substance use behaviors are learned through modeling and reinforcement processes. A primary goal of the LST curriculum is to teach adolescents both domain-specific (e.g., assertiveness skills needed to successfully withstand pressure to use substances) and generic life skills (e.g., developing personal relationships, communicating effectively) that will assist them in resisting pressures to engage in substance use behaviors and in other problem behaviors.

The LST preventive intervention was composed of three experimental conditions: a no-treatment control condition and two experimental conditions that varied based on the intensiveness of teacher training (in one condition, teachers attended a 1-day training workshop and received feedback from LST project staff [E1 group], and in the other condition, teachers were provided with a 2-hour training videotape, written instructions, and curricula materials but no feedback [E2 group]). Fifty-six participating schools in New York state were randomly assigned to one of the three conditions. During the intervention's first year, the format for the LST program involved teachers' presentation of the LST curriculum over 15 class periods to seventh graders; when students were in eighth grade, they received 10 booster sessions; and in ninth grade, they received 5 booster sessions. Students completed self-report questionnaires on their cigarette, alcohol, and marijuana use at pretest and at the end of each intervention year (at the end of seventh, eighth, and ninth grades).

In the first of two studies reviewed here, Botvin et al. (1990) tested the efficacy of the LST program by evaluating changes in outcome variables that occurred between the pretest measurement period and the measurement period following the ninth-grade intervention, comparing experimental and control groups on these variables. The results presented here are based on data collected from students who received at least 60% of the LST curriculum. Study participants were predominantly white, middle-class students coming from two-parent families. The results indicated that both experimental groups reported a significantly lower frequency of cigarette smoking and marijuana use relative to controls at the final assessment occasion. In addition, the E2 group reported a significantly lower frequency of getting drunk relative to the E1 and control groups. However, the three groups did not differ significantly on the number of times they drank alcohol or on the amount of alcohol consumed per drinking occasion.

In a second study (Botvin et al., 1995), the long-term effectiveness of the LST program was evaluated. At the end of their senior year, 6 years after the collection of baseline data, students who had previously participated in the study were asked to complete self-report questionnaires on their use of tobacco, alcohol, and marijuana. Approximately 60% of the students who participated in the pretest assessment during seventh grade completed questionnaires at the 6-year follow-up. In this study, two sets of analyses were conducted. One set included all students who completed pretest and follow-up data (full sample), and one set included students who had received at least 60% of the LST intervention and had provided pretest and follow-up data (the high fidelity sample). Results for the full sample indicated that, in general, seniors who participated in the LST program had a lower frequency of cigarette smoking, a lower frequency of getting drunk, and less polysubstance use relative to controls; however, there were no differences between program and control participants on alcohol and marijuana use variables. Results for the high fidelity sample were more promising in that they indicated that LST program participants in the high fidelity group reported significantly lower levels of cigarette, alcohol, and marijuana use and less polysubstance use relative to controls. According to Botvin et al., these findings suggest that increased exposure to the LST intervention produced greater reductions in substance use than did lower levels of exposure.

AMPS (Dielman et al., 1986;1989; Shope et al., 1992) is an alcohol-specific resistance skills training program with the aim of teaching preadolescents the behavioral skills necessary to defy peer pressures to misuse alcohol. AMPS participants included 5,635 fifth-grade and sixth-grade students from 213 classrooms within 49 schools located in six southeastern Michigan school districts. Schools were matched on several variables (students' achievement scores, SES, ethnicity) and then school buildings were randomly assigned to three study conditions: an AMPS treatment condition, an AMPS treatment plus booster sessions condition, and a no-treatment control condition. Fifth graders were included in all three groups, whereas sixth graders were included in only the AMPS treatment (with no booster sessions) and control conditions. This was because the follow-up booster sessions were conducted with half of the original fifth-grade treatment students when they were in sixth grade; thus, students who were sixth graders when the intervention was initially administered were not eligible for the later booster classes.

The study design involved pretesting students in the fall of 1984, administering the AMPS curriculum in the winter of 1985, conducting Posttest 1 in the spring of 1985 (approximately 2 months after the administration of the AMPS program), conducting the follow-up booster sessions in the winter of 1986, and collecting additional posttest data during the spring of 1986 (Posttest 2, 14-month follow-up) and the spring of 1987 (Posttest 3, 26-month follow-up). The AMPS curriculum was administered across four weekly sessions, and the follow-up booster component involved three weekly sessions; each session was 45 minutes in length (Shope et al., 1992).

In a follow-up evaluation study of the efficacy of AMPS, Dielman et al. (1989) categorized study participants into three drinking groups based on their alcohol use experiences prior to the pretest assessment. The three drinking groups included an *abstainer* group, an *adult-supervised-only* group, and a *supervised plus unsupervised* group. Supervised use indicated participants' use of alcohol within the presence of parents or other adults, and unsupervised use indicated the use of alcohol when adults were not present. A primary objective of the study was to compare study participants on their alcohol use and misuse behaviors based on their prior drinking experiences, their treatment versus control conditions, and their cross-temporal drinking behaviors (changes in drinking behaviors across the posttest measurement occasions).

Several interesting but somewhat complex findings resulted from this study. First, there were significant main effects for occasion and type of prior drinking experience for both fifth and sixth graders. (Recall that by the Posttest 3 measurement occasion, fifth graders were now seventh graders and sixth graders were now eighth graders.) Across time, both treatment and control students significantly increased their use and misuse of alcohol, and students with prior unsupervised drinking experiences had significantly higher levels of alcohol use and misuse behaviors relative to abstainers and adult-supervised-only drinkers. Second, prior drinking experience by occasion interactions were significant and showed that, across time, students with unsupervised drinking experience manifested a significantly higher rate of increase in alcohol use and misuse behaviors relative to abstainers or adult-supervised-only drinkers. Third, a significant treatment by prior drinking experience interaction among sixth graders indicated that the quantity-frequency alcohol use index averaged across all measurement occasions was significantly higher for control students who reported unsupervised drinking, relative to treatment students with prior unsupervised drinking. No differences on alcohol use behaviors were evident between control and treatment students who were either abstainers or adult-supervised-only drinkers prior to the pretest assessment.

Yet a fourth finding was a significant three-way interaction, of treatment by occasion by prior drinking experience for alcohol misuse behaviors among sixth graders. A graphical plot of this interaction showed that students who were abstainers or who experienced only adult-supervised drinking prior to the pretest showed only minimal increases in their alcohol misuse behaviors across the study interval; treatment and control students in these two drinking groups did not differ significantly on their alcohol misuse behaviors. In contrast, both control and treatment students who experienced prior unsupervised drinking had significantly higher alcohol misuse scores across the study interval than did prior abstainers or prior adult-supervised-only drinkers. Furthermore, the control condition, unsupervised drinking group had significantly greater rates of increase in their alcohol misuse behaviors from Posttest 2 to Posttest 3, relative to the treatment condition, unsupervised drinking group. No significant treatment by occasion interaction effects or three-way interaction effects were found for fifth-grade study participants.

Dielman et al. (1989) and Shope et al. (1992) proposed that there were two important aspects to be considered from their findings. First, increases in alcohol use and misuse behaviors across the 26-month study interval were minimal for the majority of study participants who had reported either no alcohol use behaviors prior to the study's inception or alcohol use behaviors only when in the presence of adults. In addition, students in these low-risk groups did not differ on their alcohol-related behaviors based on treatment-control condition status. More substantial increases in alcohol use and misuse behaviors were evident among a smaller subgroup of students who reported unsupervised use of alcohol at the pretest assessment. However, among these higher-risk adolescents, sixth-grade students in the treatment condition showed a slower rate of increase in alcohol-related behaviors relative to their control counterparts. The authors suggested that if study participants had not been grouped based on their prior alcohol use experiences, differences between control and treatment groups on their alcohol use and misuse behaviors would have been attenuated because the majority of study participants did not evidence marked increases in such behaviors. As such, the lack of significant differences between control and treatment groups would have suggested that the treatment had not been effective.

Second, program evaluation results suggested that the AMPS curriculum showed its strongest effects in reducing the rate of increase in alcohol use and misuse behaviors among sixth-grade treatment participants who had prior unsupervised alcohol use. This finding was evident in graphical plots that depicted substantial divergence in alcohol use and misuse behaviors from Posttest 2 to Posttest 3 between treatment and control subjects who reported prior unsupervised alcohol use. Taken together, these findings suggest that the AMPS was most effective in reducing the rate of increase in alcohol use and misuse behaviors among sixth graders who were exhibiting behaviors (early onset of unsupervised drinking) that potentially put them at risk for later alcohol use problems.

Preventive Interventions for High-Risk Youth

In contrast to universal programs, which include all persons in a particular population (e.g., all students in a school), selective programs target subgroups of individuals (e.g., children of alcoholics) who have a greater risk of developing a particular condition or problem (e.g., alcohol problems). Indicated prevention programs are those that target individuals manifesting specific attributes or behaviors (e.g., childhood conduct problems) that place them at high risk for development of later maladjustment (e.g., adolescent delinquent behavior; Institute of Medicine, 1994). The studies of Harrington and Donohew (1997) and Thompson, Horn, Herting, and Eggert (1997), described in the following discussions, provide two examples of indicated substance use prevention programs in that they have targeted adolescents exhibiting particular characteristics associated with increased risk for the development of substance use problems—high sensation seeking and school drop-out.

A major criticism of universal prevention programs has been their assumption of the homogeneity of substance use risk (Gorman, 1996b). For example, many universal programs have identified social pressures to use substances as *the* primary causal factor in adolescents' substance use behaviors, failing to acknowledge the multiple, complex etiologic processes that bestow differing levels of risk for the development of such behaviors (Bauman & Ennett, 1996; Catalano, Kosterman, Hawkins, Newcomb, & Abbot, 1996; Gorman, 1996b; Reed & Rountree, 1997). Targeted prevention programs acknowledge differing levels of risk; they are developed based on a theoretical understanding of the risk process and with a focus on changing those characteristics (e.g., early initiation of substance use) or circumstances (e.g., poor parenting practices) that confer increased risk for the development of substance use problems (Gorman, 1992).

The Personal Growth Class (PGC; Thompson et al., 1997) is a school-based prevention program that targets adolescents at risk for school drop-out. The program goals were threefold and include assisting adolescents (a) to reduce their involvement in substance use behaviors, (b) to improve school performance, and (c) to improve mood management (e.g., decrease depression, increase anger management skills). The two major components of the PGC curriculum were social support and life skills training, with the latter including self-esteem enhancement, decision-making skills, personal control, and interpersonal communication. Program administration occurred within the context of students' regular high school curriculum schedule, with classes meeting daily for an entire semester. For the social support component, an important task of PGC course instructors was to facilitate the development of a supportive social context by encouraging group support among class members, friendship development, and school bonding. Within this supportive context, adolescents could learn important life skills and apply their newly learned skills to the program goals of reducing substance involvement, improving mood management, and improving academic performance.

PGC program development and evaluation has been an ongoing process since 1989 (Thompson et al., 1997). Through this process, limitations of the PGC were identified, and subsequent program refinements were implemented. The study reviewed here compares *Early* cohorts, who received the original PGC curriculum, with *Late* cohorts, who received the refined PGC program, on important intervention outcomes, including measures of emotional well-being (e.g., depression, stress, self-esteem, anger), alcohol and hard drug use behaviors, and scholastic performance. The PGC curriculum was administered to 9th through 12th graders at risk for school drop-out. Approximately 90% of participants were aged 15 to 17 years. Data collection involved adolescents' completion of self-report questionnaires and collection of school records, with measurement occasions occurring at preintervention and postintervention.

Results from this study indicated that at postintervention, Late PGC participants reported significant reductions in hard drug use; significant reductions in levels of depression, perceived stress, and anger; and significant increases in self-esteem, compared with Early participants. The groups did not differ on school performance, on tobacco, alcohol, and marijuana use, and on drug use control. Based on these results, the authors suggested that, although PGC was more effective in improving emotional well-being and less effective in curbing substance use behaviors, the program effects were nevertheless important because of the potential mediating or moderating influence that mood-related factors have on substance use behaviors (e.g., adolescent substance use to self-medicate for depressed mood). As such, improvements in emotional well-being may lead to later reductions in adolescents' use of substances.

Jump Start (Harrington & Donohew, 1997) is a second example of an indicated substance use prevention program. It was developed specifically for African American adolescents who were economically disadvantaged and who were high on sensation seeking, a personality trait that has been associated with substance use behaviors among both adolescents and adults. Aspects of the social-influence model, social-skills training, and alternatives-based programs were incorporated into the program curriculum. Two primary goals of Jump Start were to assist teens in reducing their substance use behaviors and to encourage and motivate them to pursue completion of their education and career goals.

The process of developing Jump Start was an iterative one and was accomplished by repeated focus group presentations of the Jump Start curriculum to high sensation-seeking African American teens and by incorporation of their suggestions into program improvements. The activities that make up the program are geared toward appealing to high sensation-seeking youth. Data presented in the current study are from two separate program implementations (Jump Start 1 [JS1] and Jump Start 2 [JS2]). The curriculum was administered to program participants over 5 days at 4 hours per day. Data were collected at preintervention and immediate postintervention occasions, and a mail survey was conducted 60 days postintervention.

The purpose of this study was to compare low sensation seekers (LSS) and high sensation seekers (HSS) on preintervention and postintervention measures of tobacco, beer or wine, hard liquor, and marijuana use; attitudes toward substance use; and attitudes toward education. The study hypotheses were as follows: (a) At preintervention, LSS youth, relative to HSS youth, would engage in substance use behaviors less often, would view the use of substances more negatively, and would have more positive attitudes toward education; and (b) the Jump Start program would neutralize the behaviors of HSS youth, such that they would be more similar to LSS teens on the variables of interest at postintervention.

Results on the effectiveness of the Jump Start curriculum were mixed, with several important findings. First, in both the JS1 and JS2 cohorts, LSS and HSS teens differed significantly on their hard liquor and marijuana use at preintervention but not at postintervention, with HSS youth substantially reducing their use of these substances across the intervention period and becoming more similar to LSS youth. Second, among JS1 participants, the intervention did not reduce the tobacco use of HSS youth, and among JS2 participants, the intervention had only limited impact on the beer or wine use of HSS teens. Third, among JS1 teens, the HSS youth adopted substantially more negative attitudes about substance use from preintervention to postintervention assessments, thus becoming more similar to their LSS counterparts.

Family-Focused Preventive Interventions

Family-focused preventive interventions view dysfunctional interactional processes occurring within the family context as precursors of later adolescent problem behaviors, including substance use and abuse (Patterson, 1982). As such, family interventions focus on disrupting risk processes and facilitating protective processes by affecting change in variables that, based on the intervention's theoretical perspective, are hypothesized to be causally related to such processes. The research literature suggests that important *family-based risk factors* to target for change are poor socialization practices, poor supervision of the child, inconsistent disciplinary practices, poor quality of parent-child relationships, excessive family conflict, high levels of family chaos and stress, family social isolation, parental and sibling drug use, and poor parental mental health (Kumpfer, Molgaard, & Spoth, 1996). In contrast, two family-based variables that have been found to have important *protective influences* on youths' substance use behaviors are positive parent-child affective quality and effective child management practices (Dishion, Andrews, Kavanaugh, & Soberman, 1996; Spoth, Redmond, Hockaday, & Yoo, 1996).

The Iowa Strengthening Families Program (ISFP; Spoth & Redmond, 1996) is a universal, family-based prevention program adapted from the Strengthening Families Program (Kumpfer et al., 1996), a targeted intervention for high-risk families. The ISFP was one component of a larger family-based preventive intervention known as Project Family (Spoth & Redmond, 1996). A primary goal of Project Family was to teach rural families relevant skills (e.g., parenting skills) that will enhance family functioning and prevent adolescent substance use and other problem behaviors (Spoth & Redmond, 1996).

The goal of the study described in the following discussion was to evaluate the effectiveness of the ISFP on reducing or delaying adolescents' initiation of alcohol use (Spoth, Redmond, & Lepper, in press). The ISFP was based on a developmental model in that it attempted to change developmental trajectories (delay or reduce the initiation of alcohol use) among young adolescents who were at a vulnerable age to begin drinking (e.g., because of transitions from elementary to middle school) by facilitating protective processes within the family context. The intervention involved seven sessions that included parent-only, adolescent-only, and joint family groups. Parent-only sessions included training in appropriate disciplinary practices, effective communications, clarifying expectations, and managing emotions. The content of adolescent-only sessions was similar to that of the parent-only sessions but also included substance resistance and life skills training. Joint parent-adolescent sessions provided families with the opportunity to practice conflict resolution and communication skills and to build family cohesiveness.

In the larger Project Family program, 33 schools from rural communities participated, with 22 of those schools involved with the ISFP. Eleven schools were randomly assigned to the ISFP treatment condition and 11 were randomly assigned to a minimal-contact condition. Self-report questionnaires were used to assess adolescents' alcohol initiation behaviors at preintervention and postintervention (approximately 6 months after pretesting) and at 12-month and 24-month postintervention follow-ups. Participants in this study were predominantly white and from two-parent families.

Spoth et al. (in press) reported that results indicated significantly lower alcohol initiation scores for ISFP participants relative to controls at both 12-month and 24-month follow-up periods, with intervention effect sizes larger at the later follow-up. In addition to comparing the alcohol initiation scores for the ISFP and control groups, additional analyses compared the two groups on the percentage of adolescents who had not initiated alcohol use at the pretest but had initiated its use by either the 12-month or 24-month follow-ups (the percentage of new users). These analyses indicated that, at both 12-month and 24-month follow-up periods, a lower percentage of adolescents had initiated alcohol use in the ISFP condition relative to the control condition, with percentage differences between the two groups being greater at the 24-month follow-up. These findings support the efficacy of the ISFP family intervention in delaying the initiation of alcohol use behaviors among young adolescents and indicate that the program effects were stronger at the 24-month, postintervention follow-up assessment than the 12-month assessment.

Comprehensive Community Prevention Programs

Comprehensive community prevention programs focus on both *demand* and *supply* aspects of adolescent substance use (Gorman & Speer, 1996; Perry et al., 1996). Examples of prevention programs using demand reduction strategies are the Project ALERT, LST, and AMPS programs previously reviewed. These programs illustrate demand reduction approaches in that they focus on individual and interpersonal variables, such as encouraging adolescents to resist social pressures to use substances, teaching adolescents the skills to resist such pressures, and developing anti-substance-use social norms; thus, their program components are aimed at reducing teens' demands for licit and illicit substances at the individual level. In contrast, supply reduction strategies are concerned with reducing adolescents' access to substances, for example, via macro-level policies and legislation that prohibit the sale of alcohol to minors or that impose severe penalties to merchants who sell alcohol to underage teens.

It has been suggested that single-component programs (such as universal, school-based, resistance skills training programs) are too narrowly focused and ignore the multiple influences contributing to adolescent substance use (Bauman & Ennett, 1996; Catalano et al., 1996; Gorman, 1996b; Reed & Rountree, 1997). In support of this contention are recent reviews indicating that the magnitude of effects for these programs are often limited or of short duration or both (Gorman, 1995, 1996a). Pentz et al. (1989) pointed out that the short-term effectiveness of these programs may be explained, in part, by the diluting effects of environmental factors, such as family, media, and community, that are not addressed in these interventions; as such, comprehensive, multicomponent community interventions that target multiple levels of adolescents' environments (e.g., their individual, family, peer, school, community, and political contexts) are proposed as necessary to produce larger and longer-term reductions in adolescent substance use.

Two multicomponent community prevention programs are reviewed in the discussion to follow—the Midwestern Prevention Project (MPP; Pentz et al., 1989; Johnson et al., 1990) and Project Northland (Perry et al., 1996; Williams et al., in press). A primary goal of these programs has been to reduce adolescents' substance use behaviors by promoting anti-substance-use messages, practices, and norms at multiple contextual levels, including the family, school, and community (Johnson et al., 1990; Williams et al., in press).

MPP (Pentz et al., 1989; Johnson et al., 1990) is a multicomponent community program implemented in 42 Kansas City public schools from 1984 to 1986. The MPP involved five program components, including mass media coverage (newspaper articles, television news clips, radio shows), school-based educational programs (e.g., resistance skills training; joint parent-child homework assignments), parent education and organization (e.g., parents reviewing school policies), community organization (e.g., training community leaders on how to organize a substance abuse prevention task force), and policy change (Pentz et al., 1989; Johnson et al., 1990). As of the 1985/1986 school years, only the mass media and school-based programs had been implemented (Pentz et al., 1989).

Of the 42 participating schools, 8 were randomly assigned to treatment and control conditions, 20 were assigned to the treatment condition because of flexibility in their program planning, and 14 were assigned to the control condition because they were unable to reschedule their existing programming. MPP implementation was initiated during the sixth or seventh grades, depending on which year marked students' transition from elementary school to middle school or junior high school. Baseline assessments of adolescents' self-reported substance use were collected approximately 1.5 months before program administration began. The sample was racially heterogeneous.

Pentz et al. (1989) evaluated MPP effectiveness 1 year after program initiation by comparing changes between experimental and control groups from baseline to 1-year follow-up on their self-reported cigarette, alcohol, and marijuana use. These analyses indicated that, for each of these substances, both groups reported increases in use; however, the rate of increase was greater for control participants relative to program participants. That is, the change in the proportion of cigarette, alcohol, and marijuana users between preintervention and 1-year follow-up was significantly greater for adolescents in the control condition relative to the program condition. In a 3-year follow-up study (when study participants were in 9th and 10th grades) using data from students in the 8 randomly assigned schools, Johnson et al. (1990) found that the percentage of students reporting substance use behaviors had once again increased for both experimental and control groups, with a higher percentage of control students reporting use of cigarettes and marijuana relative to program students. The percentage of students using alcohol at the 3-year follow-up was approximately equal (33.8% of students in the program schools and 32.6% of students in the control schools).

Project Northland is an ongoing alcohol-specific, multicomponent, community prevention program aimed at preventing young adolescents' alcohol use (Perry et al., 1996; Williams et al., in press). It is composed of four program components, including school-based behavioral curricula (e.g., resistance skills training, joint parent-child homework exercises), peer leadership (e.g., peer leaders planning alcohol-free activities), parent involvement (e.g., parents' involvement in community task forces), and community changes (e.g., passage of legislation aimed at reducing alcohol sales to underaged teens, strengthening ties between local businesses and schools; Williams et al., in press).

There were 20 school districts in rural, northeast Minnesota that participated in Project Northland, with 10 districts randomly assigned to the intervention condition and 10 districts randomly assigned to the reference (delayed program) condition. The intervention was implemented in schools and adjoining communities between 1991 and 1994, when the adolescents were in sixth, seventh, and eighth grades. Self-report data on tobacco, alcohol, and other drug use were collected at baseline and at yearly follow-ups in 1992, 1993, and 1994. The study participants were predominantly white and lower middle class to middle class.

Perry et al. (1996) formed four groups on the basis of their baseline (sixth grade) alcohol use behaviors: *intervention baseline nonusers* (IBN), *intervention baseline users* (IBU), *reference baseline nonusers* (RBN), and *reference baseline users* (RBU). This categorization was derived because, despite random assignment of schools, students in the intervention schools reported higher levels of alcohol use at baseline relative to students in the reference schools. In comparisons between IBN and RBN groups at the 3-year follow-up, results indicated that the IBN students, relative to the RBN students, reported significantly less alcohol use in the past month and past week and significantly less cigarette and marijuana use. The groups did not differ on their ratings of perceived access to alcohol.

In contrast to these findings, there were no significant differences between the IBU and RBU groups on any of the substance use measures at the 3-year follow-up, although IBU participants reported nonsignificantly lower levels of alcohol and cigarette use. These findings suggest that the Project Northland intervention was more effective in reducing alcohol use behaviors among baseline nonusers and only minimally effective among baseline users. Additional analyses indicated that Project Northland was effective in promoting anti-substance-use attitudes, beliefs, and norms among intervention participants.

In a separate study, Williams et al. (in press) investigated Project Northland's impact on more serious alcohol use and family and school problems as assessed with five scales from the Minnesota Multiphasic Personality Inventory-Adolescent (MMPI-A). The scales included the Alcohol/Drug Problem Proneness Scale, the Alcohol/Drug Problem Acknowledgment Scale, the Adolescent-Family Problems Scale, the Adolescent-School Problems Scale, and the Adolescent-Low Aspirations Scale. As with the previous study reviewed (Perry et al., 1996), study participants were categorized into four groups based on their baseline alcohol use status: *intervention baseline nonusers* (IBN), *intervention baseline users* (IBU), *reference baseline nonusers* (RBN), and *reference baseline users* (RBU). Using these data, two sets of analyses were performed. In the first set, intervention and reference nonusers and users were compared on their MMPI-A scores at baseline and at each of the 3 years during the intervention. Notably, there were no significant differences among IBN and RBN groups on their MMPI-A scores at the baseline assessment, but at the 3-year follow-up, RBNs, relative to IBNs, reported significantly higher scores on the alcohol-drug problem proneness, alcohol-drug problem acknowledgment, family problems, and school problems subscales. In contrast, there were no statistically significant differences between the IBU and RBU groups at baseline or follow-up periods, although the IBU group tended to have lower scores on all five MMPI-A subscales.

In the second set of analyses, adolescents in the intervention and reference conditions were categorized into lower and higher risk groups based on normal or elevated MMPI-A scores measured at the 1991 baseline. For these four groups (*higher risk reference; higher risk intervention; lower risk reference; lower risk intervention*), alcohol use was compared across the four occasions of measurement—1991 baseline, 1992, 1993 and 1994. Results indicated that across the intervention period, past-month and past-week alcohol use increased for all four groups. However, there were trends for the lower and higher risk reference groups to have greater increases in alcohol use relative to the lower and higher risk intervention groups, with the only statistically significant finding being that the lower risk intervention group reported the least amount of past-month alcohol use at the 1994 assessment. As with the findings reported by Perry et al. (1996), Williams et al. (in press) concluded that Project Northland appeared to be more effective with adolescents who had not yet initiated alcohol use by sixth grade. They noted, however, that small sample sizes for adolescents who had initiated alcohol use at baseline may have compromised their ability to detect significant differences between intervention and reference groups. The authors further indicated that Project Northland, in addition to reducing alcohol-related behaviors among the baseline nonuser intervention participants, also reduced difficulties in their family and school domains, suggesting a more generalized intervention effect.

Prevention Program Summary

Despite a proliferation of adolescent substance use prevention programs, rates of teens' substance use behaviors have been increasing in recent years (University of Michigan, 1997). Gorman and colleagues provided reviews of universal, school-based (Gorman, 1995; 1996a; 1996b; 1998), and communitywide (Aguirre-Molina & Gorman, 1996; Gorman & Speer, 1996) substance use prevention programs. These reviews delineated the strengths and limitations of existing programs and were critical of universal, school-based curricula for a number of reasons, including narrow program focus (e.g., focusing only on peer pressure), an assumption of homogeneity of risk or vulnerability (a failure to recognize that different adolescents are at different levels of risk for substance use for different reasons), minimal and short-term program effects, and problems with attrition. In general, Gorman concluded that existing prevention programs have been only minimally effective in reducing adolescent substance use.

Spoth et al. (in press) have also discussed several limitations of existing family-based substance use prevention programs, including a lack of well-designed evaluation studies, subject attrition, and methodological shortcomings (e.g., experimental group inequivalence, inadequate statistical power). West and Aiken (1997) discussed the need for evaluation of the program effects (e.g., helpful, harmful, neutral) of specific components within multi-component programs.

My brief review of prevention studies expands on the foregoing discussion and suggests several limitations of existing prevention programs. First, most of the programs were more effective in reducing adolescents' use of cigarettes and marijuana and less effective in reducing their alcohol use behaviors (Botvin et al., 1990; Ellickson & Bell, 1990; Johnson et al., 1990). Ellickson and Bell (1990) suggested that reductions in adolescents' use of alcohol may be difficult to obtain because of societal attitudes and media messages that are more condoning of drinking behaviors. Comprehensive community-wide programs, such as MPP and Project Northland, have been developed to promote anti-substance-use attitudes, expectations, and behaviors within multiple domains of adolescents' lives, including peers, family, the school, and the community, with the ultimate goal of making the nonuse of cigarettes, alcohol, and other drugs the normative behavior among adolescents.

Second, the findings from several studies (e.g., Ellickson & Bell, 1990; Perry et al., 1996) indicated stronger program effects for baseline nonusers and virtually no program effects for adolescents who had an earlier onset of substance use behaviors and who therefore may be at greater risk for later substance use problems. A notable exception to these findings were results from the AMPS study (Dielman et al., 1989), which showed that the intervention was most effective in reducing the rate of increase in alcohol misuse behaviors among sixth-grade participants who reported early onset, unsupervised drinking. An important criticism of universal prevention programs has been their assumption of homogeneity of substance use risk (Gorman, 1996b). The general findings that universal, school-based prevention programs are more effective for lower-risk adolescents and less effective for higher-risk adolescents, along with the findings of other researchers that have indicated differing developmental pathways to substance use (Duncan, Tildesley, Duncan, & Hops, 1995), indicate differing levels of risk among adolescents. These findings suggest a need for the identification of adolescents at higher risk for substance-use-related problems and for the development of targeted prevention programs designed to meet their unique needs. Two targeted programs reviewed here—PGC (Thompson et al., 1997) and Jump Start (Harrington & Donohew, 1997)—were developed specifically for targeted groups of at-risk adolescents, and evaluation studies indicated some success in meeting program goals.

Third, two programs—Project ALERT (Ellickson et al., 1993) and LST (Botvin et al., 1995)—were evaluated for their long-term effects on reducing or preventing adolescent substance use, with results indicating decay of program effectiveness for Project ALERT and more success for the LST program but only for those participants exposed to at least 60% of the intervention. Based on results such as these, a number of researchers have suggested that adolescent substance use prevention programs should be comprehensive (target multiple domains of children's functioning; Pentz et al., 1989), begin before the onset of substance use behaviors—and given the earlier onset of such behaviors among a number of adolescents, this suggests program implementation should begin with young children (Williams et al., in press), be of longer duration (Ellickson et al., 1993), and be designed to maximize adolescents' program exposure (Botvin et al., 1995).

Despite these limitations, improvements in prevention programs and evaluation are evident. For example, Project Family (Spoth & Redmond, 1996; Spoth, Redmond & Shin, 1998) is a theory-based substance use preventive intervention for rural families aimed at ameliorating risk processes and promoting protective processes. It was developed based on substantive gaps and methodological shortcomings identified in the extant literature (Spoth & Redmond, 1996). A focus of this ongoing research project has been to conduct methodologically sound program evaluations investigating the intervention's efficacy by comparing intervention and control group outcomes and by identifying factors influencing families' participation in the intervention (Spoth & Redmond, 1996). It is important that the Project Family researchers have been using the program's prospective, longitudinal data and advanced statistical data analytic techniques, such as structural equation modeling, to model individual, family, and intervention effects on program outcomes by modeling hypothesized mediating processes (Spoth et al., 1996, 1998). Such preventive interventions, guided by theory and solid research designs, are likely to increase our knowledge of what works and what doesn't and what accounts for changes in behavioral outcomes, such as reductions in alcohol use or age of initiation.

SOCIAL POLICY INTERVENTIONS

Previously discussed intervention approaches have focused on individual characteristics (e.g., attitudes toward alcohol use), parent-child interactions (e.g., enhanced communication), peer relations (e.g., peer resistance skills training), and community members (e.g., teachers, police) and institutions (e.g., the media) to modify substance use behaviors among adolescents. In addition to these efforts, there have been attempts to evaluate the impact of changes in social policies on drinking practices and well-being (e.g., morbidity and mortality) among adolescents. Although these approaches are less psychologically oriented than those described previously, it is important to recognize the importance of such social policies in regulating the range of legally permissible, and functionally probable, drinking behaviors among adolescents. That is, social policies such as reducing the minimum drinking age or increasing the price of alcohol via taxes, act in a probabilistic manner to foster or deter alcohol-related behaviors via constraints on the natural ecologies of drinking behavior. Hence, social-policy questions arise, such as, will there be a reduction in fatal automobile crashes among youth if the minimum drinking age is 21 years instead of 18 years? Do zero-tolerance laws affect drinking-and-driving behavior among youth? Does the price of alcohol, which may be influenced by an increase in taxes on alcohol, result in a reduction of alcohol-related behaviors among youth?

Alcohol Taxes

Several studies, usually conducted by economists, have examined the relationship between tax-related increases on alcohol and indicators of potential changes in adolescent drinking behaviors. Many such studies have used "pre and post" research designs and evaluated changes in official state record statistics, such as traffic fatalities, or annual self-report national survey data after increases in taxes on alcohol. Some findings have indicated that increases in beer prices were associated with a reduction in the frequency of alcohol consumption and heavy drinking episodes among youth, for example (Coate & Grossman, 1988; Grossman, Coate, & Arluck, 1987). Similarly, higher taxes on beer have been associated with a reduction in traffic crash fatalities among young drivers (Saffer & Grossman, 1987).

In a detailed study of price sensitivity of alcoholic beverages and adolescent alcohol use, Grossman et al. (1987) reported two quite interesting findings. First, based on their analyses of data from 790 youths (aged 16-21 years) participating in the National Health and Nutrition Examination Survey, Grossman et al. concluded that a dime increase in the price of beer would contribute to a decrease in the number of youth drinking by approximately 11%; a 30-cent increase in the price of liquor would contribute to a decrease in the number of youth drinking by approximately 23%. Hence, the impact of price increases on alcohol beverages may be quite substantial with regard to the prevalence of users and to a reduction in mortality. A second interesting finding was that the impact of price increases (via taxes) and increases in the legal drinking age (to be discussed more thoroughly) were associated with different individual drinking styles. The data suggested that frequent beer drinkers were more influenced by legal-drinking-age changes than infrequent beer drinkers but that infrequent beer drinkers were more influenced by price than frequent beer drinkers. Thus, these data suggest that alcohol taxation is a viable social policy option that may affect some features of adolescent alcohol use but also that policy changes may not yield constant or equally effective benefits across all youthful drinkers.

Minimum Legal Drinking Age

The U.S. Constitution—specifically, the 21st Amendment, which repealed Prohibition—provided states with the legal authority to regulate most aspects of alcohol commerce (e.g., licensing, advertising, determining who may drink alcohol). This contributed to the nonuniformity of the minimum legal drinking age (MLDA) across states and to a host of associated difficulties with adolescent drinking practices (adolescents crossing state lines to purchase alcohol, increases in alcohol-related crash fatalities on bridges and by-ways across state lines). Furthermore, the emerging data indicated that the risk of an alcohol-related fatal crash among individuals under age 21 was greater because of less experience in driving an automobile and the tendency, in the aggregate, to take more risks while driving, such as speeding or failing to wear seat belts (Hingson, Heeren, & Winter, 1996). In 1984, the Federal Uniform Drinking Age Act was enacted, and it encouraged all states to adopt the MLDA of 21; failure to comply with this request would result in a loss of portions of the state's Federal Highway Trust Fund share. All 50 states complied by 1988.

Research on the usefulness of this MLDA policy has generally supported reductions in adolescent alcohol-related outcomes by comparing data before and after implementation of the age-21 MLDA program. For example, several studies have reported reductions in youth alcohol consumption, traffic crashes, and related fatalities subsequent to the age-21 MLDA (Hingson et al., 1994; Wagenaar, 1993). Traffic crashes among youth were reduced by about 15% in some states, and alcohol-related traffic deaths declined by 59% between 1982 and 1995—from 5,380 to 2,201 cases (Hingson et al., 1996). The National Highway Traffic Safety Administration estimated that the age-21 MLDA policy prevented 1,071 traffic crash fatalities in 1987 alone. In a follow-up study of a nationwide cohort of high school seniors, O'Malley and Wagenaar (1991) reported that the age-21 MLDA policy not only reduced alcohol consumption for this sample during their senior year but was also associated with lower levels of alcohol use at age 25, when drinking was legal.

Zero-Tolerance Laws

Zero-tolerance laws set the maximum blood alcohol concentration limits for drivers under age 21 to 0.02% or lower, in essence, conveying the message that individuals under age 21 should not drink at all and then drive, lest they suffer fairly severe legal penalties. The National Highway Systems Act provides financial incentives for states to adopt zero-tolerance laws, and at least 37 states and the District of Columbia have complied (Hingson et al., 1996). In an initial study of 12 states that adopted zero-tolerance laws and nearby 12 states that did not, findings indicated a 20% reduction in single-vehicle, nighttime, fatal crashes among 15-year-old to 20-year-old drivers in the zero-tolerance states (Hingson et al., 1994). This policy is still relatively new, and future studies will need to replicate and extend the available information on zero-tolerance laws, but the initial findings do support a significant decrease in single-vehicle, nighttime, fatal crashes among youth.

TREATMENT APPROACHES

On the basis of data collected in 1991, it was estimated that about 6% of patients in alcoholism and drug treatment units were under the age of 18 years (U.S. Department of Health and Human Services, 1993). Of this 6%, 35% were treated for alcohol disorders and 40% for alcohol and drug disorders. Service programs consisted of over 3,000 specialized programs for youth in outpatient, day treatment, residential, and hospitalization settings. There is a broad range of approaches that have been used in these settings, including the 12-step model, behavioral interventions, family therapy, and educational and vocational assistance and rehabilitation (Bukstein, 1994).

Perhaps the most widely used inpatient approach is the 28-day, group-oriented Minnesota model that relies on the 12-step program of recovery (Wheeler & Malmquist, 1987). This program consists of several components, including group meetings (e.g., Alcoholics Anonymous), educational presentations about alcoholism and associated health and social problems, group counseling, family therapy, and the completion of workbooks by adolescents to monitor personal progress and to evaluate ongoing feelings and reactions about their alcohol disorders. This multifaceted approach is designed to provide a supportive setting that simultaneously addresses personal and family problems, as well as educating adolescents about the adverse consequences associated with substance use and abuse. Behavioral intervention approaches have also been used with adolescents in treatment facilities. These interventions have often focused on skills training (e.g., refusal skills, problem-solving skills, anger control, leisure-time management) and relapse prevention. The objectives of the skills training methods are to build up the coping capacities, social competencies, and life skills of adolescents to more adequately manage their lives in a more constructive fashion than relying on alcohol or drugs.

A range of different family therapy approaches has also been used with adolescent substance abusers. This includes behavioral family interventions, such as parent management training and contingency contracting. Such family interventions focus on the training for specific skills (e.g., parenting skills, parent-adolescent communication skills) and the establishment of agreed-on rules of behavior and their consequences between adolescents and their parents. Family systems (or systemic) therapies have also been used with substance-abusing adolescents in treatment to address issues surrounding intergenerational conflict, family alliances, boundary conditions, and so forth. These family therapies involve an analysis of the dynamic relationships among family members and how given dynamics may have contributed to and may change adolescent substance abuse. In addition to these family therapies, a number of programs include educational and vocational assistance or rehabilitation. Some long-term adolescent inpatient programs incorporate a variety of the approaches described previously, including AA meetings, group sessions, family therapy, physical health and nutrition programs, and school and vocational assistance.

Although a number of therapeutic approaches have been used with substance-abusing adolescents, firm conclusions about their respective treatment efficacies and posttreatment clinical courses are lacking for several reasons. First, many of the therapeutic applications have occurred without scientific data collected to facilitate an evaluation of the treatment effects. Second, many of the existing studies have examined treatment outcome in a more global manner (e.g., in relation to relapse) rather than looking at the efficacy of given treatment approaches (for a review, see Brown, 1993). Third, Bukstein (1994) reports that many of the treatment outcome studies completed with adolescent substance abusers contained scientific flaws (e.g., absence of a control group, weak or inconsistent baseline data collection, low retention across time) that deter more confident conclusions about the findings. Fourth, many of the current estimates of adolescent treatment outcomes are based on samples from settings that included both adults and adolescents; hence, treatment efficacy and posttreatment clinical course may differ in settings that are oriented toward adolescents only (Brown, 1993). Fifth, treatment outcome studies define *relapse* in different ways (e.g., having one drink, returning to pretreatment drinking levels) and focus on one (e.g., alcohol) or several (any illicit substance) relapse variables.

Brown, Vik, and Creamer (1989) provided data on relapse rates for substance abuse among adolescents in the initial 6 months subsequent to treatment. The relapse rate for alcohol abuse was approximately 40% at 6 months, and within 1 year, almost 85% of the sample relapsed for one or more addictive substances. These rates are highly similar to those reported with adult substance abusers. Catalano, Hawkins, Wells, Miller, and Brewer (1991) conducted a review of factors that predicted adolescent relapse and lack of relapse to alcohol use subsequent to treatment. Factors that predicted noncompletion of treatment included a younger age of alcohol onset, more severe alcohol use at baseline, multiple substance use, deviant behavior, and criminal involvement. Thoughts, feelings, and cravings about alcohol, reduced school or work involvement, and less satisfactory leisure time activities were posttreatment predictors of relapse. Better treatment outcomes were associated with time spent in treatment, staff characteristics (e.g., staff attitudes and level of training), the availability of special services, and family participation.

Pharmacologic Treatment

The pharmacologic treatment of adult alcohol disorders was recently invigorated by the approval from the Federal Drug Administration (FDA) of naltrexone. Naltrexone is the first FDA-approved pharmacologic agent for alcoholism in over 50 years. It has been proposed that naltrexone affects underlying motivational systems (e.g., craving alcohol) via serotonin regulation to reduce the desire to drink. In short, the consumption of alcohol is not as reinforcing to pleasure centers in the brain when individuals are taking naltrexone. This reinforcement reduction approach to decreasing alcohol craving and pleasure contrasts sharply with the other major FDA-approved pharmacologic agent for alcoholism—disulfiram (Antabuse). The use of disulfiram relies on aversive conditioning in that this pharmacologic agent inhibits the liver enzyme aldehyde dehydrogenase, which catalyzes the oxidation of aldehyde to acetate. The upshot of this process is the accumulation of acetaldehyde in the body, which in turn contributes to symptoms such as nausea, headaches, and so forth. Among adults, there has been limited success with the use of disulfiram (Alterman, O'Brien, & McLellan, 1991); research on the therapeutic efficacy of naltrexone has yet to be completed.

Pharmacologic agents, such as disulfiram or naltrexone, have not been used among adolescents with alcohol disorders and hence have not been evaluated for efficacy (e.g., Kaminer, 1995). The reasons for this are multiple, including (a) incomplete information on the pharmacokinetics, side effects, and dose-response relationships of these agents for adolescents, who vary in their rates of physical and cognitive growth; (b) a fear among some parents that the use of pharmaceutical agents will only perpetuate substance-abusing tendencies among their troubled adolescents; and (c) antimedication sentiments for children and adolescents expressed by some media and religious groups (Biderman, 1992). Despite the absence of the use of these alcohol-specific pharmacologic agents with adolescents, pharmacologic agents have been used with adolescents with alcohol and substance abuse disorders and co-occurring psychiatric disorders (Bukstein, 1994; Kaminer, 1995). Antidepressants, lithium, and other psychotropic medications are being used increasingly with adolescents with comorbid substance abuse and psychiatric disturbance. Some initial, small sample findings suggest an association between treatment completion (versus dropping out of treatment) and use of psychotropic medication among adolescent substance abusers (Kaminer, Tarter, Bukstein, & Kabene, 1992). However, conduct disorder was also more prevalent among the dropouts and mood disorders among the completers, so the treatment efficacy findings may have been influenced more by comorbid condition than by the use of medication. More refined research designs will be required in future investigations of the therapeutic effectiveness of psychotropic medications for substance-abusing adolescents.

In summary, the pharmacologic treatment of adolescents with alcohol and other substance abuse disorders has not been systematically practiced or evaluated scientifically. There have been some recent efforts and proposals to evaluate the efficacy of pharmacologic agents used for other adolescent co-occurring disorders, such as major depressive disorder and attention-deficit disorder, for their therapeutic impact on adolescent alcohol and drug abuse (Kaminer, 1995). Furthermore, given the high rate of comorbid substance abuse and psychiatric disorders among adolescents in treatment facilities and the high rates of relapse among adolescent substance abusers (Catalano et al.,1991), there is increasing interest in the potential efficacy of combination, or multiple, treatment strategies (McLellan, Arndt, Metzger, Woody, & O'Brien, 1993). An important area of future research will be a more systematic evaluation of pharmacological agents (preferably in conjunction with other treatment modalities) on adolescent substance abuse, psychiatric functioning, and general life adjustment (e.g., school completion, coping and social-skill development). Should naltrexone prove effective with adult alcoholic samples, future research with older adolescents may be warranted, to evaluate the efficacy of this pharmacological agent for this age group. Likewise, secondary gains of medications used to treat other disorders (e.g., psychotropic medications for major depressive disorder) among adolescents should be investigated for influences on alcohol and drug use problems.

SUMMARY

In the past 20 years or so, there has been a profusion of intervention programs and legal and social policies aimed at the reduction of adolescent alcohol and substance use and associated adverse consequences (e.g., fatal crashes, violence and victimization). Some psychosocial preventive interventions have had some success in reducing levels of substance use among adolescents. However, these programs have usually been limited in three significant ways. First, the primary reduction in substance use has tended to be short term. Subsequent to the cessation of the intervention, those adolescents who had reduced their use of substances had caught up to their same-age cohort who had not reduced their use. This clearly suggests the need for ongoing booster sessions to maintain the desired reductions in substance use. The exact number of booster sessions required, the content of the booster sessions, intervention features (e.g., staff training), and so forth need to be systematically evaluated to determine optimally efficient ongoing interventions. Second, preventive interventions have been less effective in reducing alcohol use relative to other substances (e.g., cigarettes, marijuana), perhaps because of societal behaviors and attitudes that are more condoning of alcohol use. Third, the primary reduction in substance use has been associated principally with those at the light-use rather than heavy-use portion of the substance use spectrum. Therefore, universal, school-based preventive interventions appear to be least effective with those at greatest risk for subsequent serious alcohol-related and substance-related problems, including substance use disorders. The matching of adolescents manifesting more serious substance use problems may require more intensive and extensive interventions to consistently affect their current levels of use and prevent the escalation to more serious use.

The implementation of legal and social policies has had a significant impact on adolescent alcohol use in some domains. For example, alcohol-related automobile crashes and fatalities among youth have decreased substantially with the passing of minimum age drinking laws. Likewise, changes in the price of alcohol have had an impact on adolescent alcohol consumption. Such changes in legal, economic, and social policies toward adolescent drinking are clearly needed as part of a matrix of interventions designed to modify adolescent alcohol use and reduce the associated risk of health-compromising outcomes for adolescents, their families, and society at large.

On the basis of the limited existing data on treatment and posttreatment course with adolescent alcohol and drug abusers, it is evident that much research remains to be completed to adequately serve the needs of our youth. Current evidence is inconclusive regarding the relative efficacy of alternative approaches to treatment (e.g., AA versus cognitive-behavioral therapy) and their posttreatment consequences. The evidence that is available (e.g., Brown, 1993) suggests that relapse rates for adolescents are as high as they are for adults, with a large portion relapsing within a few months of exiting from treatment. Longer and more intensive aftercare interventions may be needed with adolescents subsequent to treatment to maintain any positive gains of the treatment.

5

CONCEPTUAL AND METHODOLOGICAL ISSUES AND FUTURE RESEARCH DIRECTIONS

The previous chapters in this book have attempted to provide representative coverage of the research literature relevant to adolescent alcohol use. Much of the material presented was more descriptive than critical, though weaknesses and limitations of specific studies or specific research domains were identified. In this chapter, some larger conceptual and methodological issues are presented that confront researchers and health care providers who are addressing concerns about adolescent alcohol use and abuse. The chapter has three sections: (a) conceptual issues, (b) issues pertaining to risk and protective factors, and (c) issues about prevention and treatment.

CONCEPTUAL ISSUES

As described in Chapter 1, there have been a number of different theoretical and conceptual models proposed to account for adolescent alcohol use. However, many of these theories and models have been somewhat restricted in scope. For example, key variables associated with some of the theories are significantly related to adolescent alcohol use but are of small magnitude with respect to accounting for individual variation in alcohol outcomes. In addition, these variables are equally predictive of a wide range of behaviors and thus indicate little specificity with regard to the prediction of alcohol-related behaviors in particular. There have also been a limited number of competing tests of alternative theories and models. Perhaps even more revealing and important, much of the extant theorizing and model building has been geared toward a more descriptive (versus explanatory) phase of research in identifying the multiple factors that are involved in the prediction of adolescent alcohol use and abuse. It is evident that multiple factors will need to be specified to account for individual variation in adolescent alcohol use, rather than one or two major factors. Three critical issues that need to be addressed to more finely tune theorizing to advance the field of adolescent alcohol use study relate to (a) a greater appreciation of adolescent development and its attendant life tasks; (b) an increasing role for the specification and evaluation of prospective, multiple mediator models; and (c) the conceptualization of alcohol phenotypes (e.g., quantity and frequency of use, binge drinking, alcohol problems) as unique outcomes or as one of several problem behaviors with a common etiology and time course. Each of these issues is discussed in the following pages.

Importance of Adolescent Development

Alcohol use in adolescence (and other portions of the lifespan) does not occur in a vacuum but rather is embedded within ongoing life course trajectories of individuals confronting a range of age-salient life tasks (Erikson, 1963). Among the age-salient tasks confronted by adolescents are changes associated with biological processes (e.g., onset of puberty, substantial increases in physical size), shifts away from the family and toward peers for some activities, the development of intimate relationships with a significant other, negotiating balances between autonomy and relatedness in the family, and adapting to changes in school settings, from relatively small, more personal elementary school settings to larger, less personal secondary school settings (Schulenberg, Maggs, & Hurrelmann, 1997). Relatedly, research has also indicated that adolescence is the peak period in the lifespan for the occurrence of stressful life events (Newcomb, Huba, & Bentler, 1981).

The role of alcohol use in adolescence may be more usefully guided conceptually and methodologically by recognizing this array of ongoing stressors and adaptational demands in adolescence and more closely linking hypothesized relationships for alcohol initiation, escalation, or termination with these age-normative challenges. Baumrind and Moselle (1985), for example, have proposed that earlier-onset substance use among adolescents is detrimental to young adult development. This occurs because early substance use and abuse by adolescents undermines their ability to successfully negotiate the tasks of adolescence, and hence they lag developmentally in their confrontation with the age-salient tasks of young adulthood. Baumrind and Moselle suggest, for instance, that genuine intimacy and authentic interpersonal communication may lack appropriate depth and commitment when adolescents are abusing substances. This occurs because a reliance on mind-altering substances by teens may undermine cognitive growth (e.g., away from egocentrism) and a secure sense of personal identity that facilitates engagement in intimate relationships.

Findings by Magnusson (1988) have also indicated that individual variation in the timing of age-normative events may influence alcohol use. He reported that early-maturing girls (based on pubertal status) were more likely to engage in early alcohol initiation than later-maturing girls. The proposed mechanism to account for this finding was that the peer groups of earlier-maturing girls were older and more involved in substance use and other deviant activities than the peer groups of later-maturing girls. In essence, individual variation in an age-normative biological event (onset of puberty) was associated with social factors (peer group selection and socialization) that accounted for variation in levels of adolescent alcohol use for girls who were the same age.

Future research on adolescent alcohol use may benefit from hypotheses about ongoing, bidirectional relationships between salient developmental tasks and adolescent alcohol use. That is, developmental changes may influence higher levels of alcohol use (e.g., establishing stronger peer relationships), and higher levels of alcohol use may impede the successful resolution of some life tasks. For example, individual variation in the resolution of family autonomy and relatedness may be influenced by actions and reactions of parents and adolescents to adolescent peer activity and alcohol use. Heightened parent-adolescent conflict may impede the successful resolution of this task, whereas constructive, shared problem solving may facilitate its resolution. The use of theories of adolescent development may offer a strong theoretical backdrop for more precise theories and hypotheses about adolescent alcohol use.

Prospective Multiple Mediator Models

Findings from the literature on risk and protective factors (e.g., Hawkins et al., 1992) have clearly identified a large number of influential factors for adolescent alcohol use. There has been a growing recognition of the need to model the simultaneous contribution of these multiple factors through carefully specified models that are posed to account for the processes contributing to adolescent alcohol use (e.g., Chassin et al., 1993; Sher, 1991; Wills et al., 1998). Sher (1991) and others (e.g., Haynes, 1992) have expanded the framework of Baron and Kenny (1986) to suggest that multiple-mediator models be specified and evaluated to assess the plausibility of posited explanatory process models that account for variation in outcome variables, such as adolescent alcohol use. Several such models have been used in the area of adolescent substance use (e.g., Chassin et al., 1993; Wills et al., 1998), and future research in the field of adolescent alcohol use would benefit from more extensive use of such models. In addition, mediator models are especially useful in evaluating the plausibility of presumed causal relations with prospective data, where control over temporal parameters may facilitate the feasibility of hypothesized relations.

Alcohol Use: Unique Phenotypes or Components of General Problem Behaviors?

Problem Behavior Theory (PBT; Jessor et al., 1991; Jessor & Jessor, 1977) provides a quite parsimonious and useful approach for describing a pattern of positive correlations across a wide range of behaviors during adolescence, including alcohol and drug use, delinquency, sexual activity, and poor school performance. PBT has served as a catalyst over the past 25 years for recognizing the multiproblem nature of troubled youth and the need for interventionists and health care providers to incorporate this information into their treatment and service plans.

However, the adequacy of PBT to account for problem behaviors among adolescents has been questioned on several fronts in recent years. First, the factor analysis of multiple problems (e.g., alcohol use, drug use, delinquency) has not yielded a clear, one-factor solution (Gillmore, Hawkins, Catalano, Day, & Moore, 1991; McGee & Newcomb, 1992; Osgood, Johnston, O'Malley, & Bachman, 1988), thus bringing into question the notion of a single underlying problem behavior dimension. Second, numerous studies focused on individual-level data (versus aggregated data describing a sample) have indicated diversification with respect to problem behaviors (e.g., Loeber, Farrington, Stouthamer-Loeber, & Van Kammen, 1998; Elliott, Huizinga, & Menard, 1989). For example, some adolescents who are abusing alcohol are not abusing other illicit substances (e.g., cocaine); some adolescents who are performing poorly in school are not abusing any substances; some adolescents are heavy smokers and are depressed, but they are abusing neither alcohol nor other illicit drugs. These findings are consistent with the adolescent substance abuse literature, where there are multiple, unique patterns of coexisting psychiatric disorders (e.g., alcohol abuse and depressive disorder, alcohol abuse and conduct disorder; Bukstein, Brent, & Kaminer, 1989; Clark, Jacob, & Mezzich, 1994.).

Third, prospective studies of adolescents have yielded heterogeneity with regard to correlates, predictors, and future outcomes of problem behaviors. For example, findings by Schulenberg et al. (1996) indicated that adolescents similarly identified as serious binge drinkers in adolescence had quite variable outcomes in young adulthood contingent on a range of other personality and attitudinal variables exhibited during adolescence. As such, knowledge of binge drinking as a problem behavior was not sufficiently informative to predict future outcomes or to serve as a solid basis for proposed interventions. Similarly, Tubman, Windle, and Windle (1996) reported that the relationship between sexual onset (the time of first sexual intercourse) and delinquency was contingent on the timing of sexual debut. Sexual onset was associated with increases in general levels of delinquency only if onset occurred when adolescents were younger (around ages 14-16 years); sexual onset that occurred later (around ages 17-19 years) was not associated with increases in general levels of delinquency. These findings were attributable to possibly greater maturity on the part of older adolescents in selecting romantic (versus casual) partners and in higher levels of cognitive functioning to cope psychologically with sexual relationships. In relation to PBT, these findings suggest that the relationship between two presumed problem behaviors varies according to adolescents' age, their level of maturity, and possibly the nature of the relationship (and other contextual variables); hence, the generality of PBT appears limited for describing temporally dynamic relations that are unfolding across time. Subsequent research on adolescent alcohol use may benefit by considering both the generality and specificity of multiple problem behaviors and the generality and specificity of predictors and consequences of these problem behaviors.

In addition, although various indicators of adolescent alcohol use (e.g., quantity and frequency of use, binge drinking, alcohol problems) are significantly correlated, they are not identical phenotypes (e.g., Windle, 1996). Alcohol initiation, quantity and frequency of use, binge drinking, and alcohol problems may have the same or different (or some overlapping) predictors and consequences. Similarly, there is increasing recognition of patterns of co-occurring problems and comorbid disorders among adolescents in treatment settings (e.g., Bukstein et al., 1989), but little research has been directed toward common and unique precursors of alcohol use versus cocaine use versus major depressive disorders, or differences in the temporal ordering of onset for these disorders, or the implications of comorbid alcohol and depressive disorders for preventive interventions. It appears, for example, that dysfunctional family processes (e.g., poor parenting skills, marital conflict) are associated with a range of problematic outcomes among adolescents. However, are the family dynamics the same across different adolescent problem conditions, or are some problems, such as with adolescents' heavier alcohol use, associated specifically with higher parental alcohol abuse and more physical and sexual violence? Also, what are the long-term effects (e.g., on young adult alcohol and psychiatric disorders, occupational functioning) of different alcohol phenotypes manifested during adolescence? Subsequent research may benefit from a dynamic framework that considers such multifaceted questions about the specificity and generality of precursors and consequences for different alcohol phenotypes.

RISK AND PROTECTIVE FACTORS

As described in Chapter 3, there has been an extensive amount of research conducted on the identification of risk and protective factors for adolescent alcohol use. However, several issues remain to be addressed in subsequent research to optimize the contribution of this literature. These issues include (a) convergence on conceptual and statistical models to represent and test risk and protective factors, (b) using a dynamic, bidirectional-effects developmental model to evaluate risk and protective factors as influencing and being influenced by alcohol use and other problem behaviors, and (c) developing appropriate composite indexes or alternative quantitative indexes for multiple risk and multiple protective factors.

The concepts of risk and protective factors and resiliency have been used in a variety of ways in the literature (Rutter, 1987; Windle, in press), and this has often led to confusion. There is agreement that a risk factor increases the probability of the expression of a given undesirable outcome (e.g., early-onset drinking on the occurrence of an alcohol disorder). For example, based on data from adoptee and twin research designs, male offspring of alcoholics are 4 times more likely to develop alcohol disorders than are male offspring of nonalcoholics (Cloninger et al., 1981; McGue, 1994). There is also agreement that protective factors function in just the opposite manner, that is, to decrease the probability of the expression of a given undesirable outcome; for example, an affectionate, cuddly, socially engaging temperament style during infancy and childhood predicted healthier life course trajectories (e.g., higher levels of education, better employment opportunities, fewer health problems) among a sample of children at high risk due to parental alcoholism and low socioeconomic status (Werner & Smith, 1982).

Hence, at an abstract level, risk and protective factors may appear to be easily distinguishable according to the agreed-on definitions provided earlier, but in practice it becomes more difficult. The difficulty stems from differences in underlying model assumptions that provide the substantive context for the interpretation of risk and protective factors and the implications for resiliency. Early investigators in protective-factors research identified such variables within the context of high-risk research designs (e.g., Garmezy & Rutter, 1983; Werner & Smith, 1982). That is, given a sample at high risk for an undesirable outcome (e.g., schizophrenia, alcoholism) because of a given risk condition (e.g., low socioeconomic status, family history of a specific disorder), what factors predicted what children *did not* develop the expected disorder? This high risk model may be contrasted with a second model that I refer to as a *general-vulnerability model* in which *all children* are viewed as at some level of risk (i.e., there is individual variation in liability to risk), and factors associated with desirable outcomes (e.g., the absence of an alcohol disorder, lower levels of adolescent alcohol use) are viewed as protective.

Difficulties in distinguishing between risk and protective factors arise from the general-vulnerability model in that a given variable is defined as *risk* or *protective* contingent on the directionality of scoring for a unitary, bipolar dimension (e.g., Stouthamer-Loeber et al., 1993; Windle, in press). For example, if high family emotional support correlates positively with lower adolescent alcohol use, according to this model, it is a protective factor. However, if low family emotional support correlates positively with in- creased adolescent alcohol use, according to this model, it is a risk factor. This obviously reduces the identification and reference of family emotional support as a risk or protective factor to a mere semantic preference. In addition, in the translation of this conceptual model to a statistical model, *main effects* are sufficient to infer the risk or protectiveness of given variables contingent on their directional relationship with outcome variables.

By contrast, for the high-risk model, the protectiveness of a given factor is in relation to a specified and presumably empirically supported risk factor, such as social disadvantage or family history of psychiatric or substance abuse disorder. For example, a cuddly, affectionate temperament style was a protective factor for socially disadvantaged children of alcoholic parents because it presumably contributed to positive interactions and social re- sources that were not available to those children with a similar risk profile but less engaging personalities. Those children with an affectionate tempera- ment style had more healthy outcomes in adolescence and adulthood than those without these characteristics. In the translation of this conceptual model to a statistical model, statistically significant *interaction effects* between the hypothesized protective factor (e.g., family emotional support, affectionate temperament style) and the designated risk factor (e.g., low SES, family history of disorder) on the outcome variable(s) must be demonstrated (and be in the proper direction) to substantiate claims about its protective influences.

As many behavioral scientists attempt to develop alternative health paradigms (alternatives to a narrow-range medical disease model), these distinctions between the general vulnerability model and the high risk model are important, and difficulties arise when efforts are made to interpret empirical studies *as if* the findings based on these two models may be similarly interpreted and used to guide prevention and treatment programs. Stouthamer-Loeber et al. (1993) have wrestled with scoring procedures to distinguish risk and protective factors. Their initial research on this topic needs to be diligently followed up in the field to enhance the value of a risk and protective framework. There is a need for correspondence between conceptualization and measurement for this framework to be used as a guide to preventive interventions.

An additional limitation of current research on risk and protective factors for adolescent alcohol use and other indicators of adolescent dysfunction (e.g., drug use, mental disorders) has been the adoption of a unidirectional rather than bidirectional model of dynamic relations. That is, risk and protective factors have been viewed as causes and moderators of outcomes but not as *influenced* by outcomes such as alcohol and drug use or mental disturbance. For example, early-onset deviant behaviors, such as alcohol use or aggression, may have direct and indirect effects on potential risk and protective factors. Such early-onset behaviors may contribute to deviant labeling by significant others (e.g., teachers, peers), to affiliations with more deviant peers, and to fluctuating mood states resulting from the pharmacologic properties of substances consumed. As such, the probability that protective factors will emerge to counteract risk factors and expressed problem behaviors (e.g., alcohol use, aggression) may decrease as children and adolescents embed themselves within a more deviant lifestyle (and probable life course trajectory) and away from potential protective sources, such as family members, school counselors, or clergy. To more fully comprehend the dynamic process relations of adolescent development, it is necessary for subsequent research to consider the consequences of problem behaviors on risk and protective factors across time, as well as the mediating and moderating roles of these risk and protective factors.

Yet an additional issue to consider in the literature about risk and protective factors concerns the scoring procedures combining risk and protective factor scores to form composite scores. Several investigators (e.g., Jessor et al., 1995; Newcomb & Felix-Ortiz, 1992) have derived composite indexes of risk and protective scores by assigning scores of 0 or 1 to each of a multitude of identified factors, such as poor school performance, deviant peer affiliation, poor parent-adolescent relations, and then adding the resulting scores to form composite indexes of risk and protectiveness. Such derived composite indexes may provide a parsimonious quantitative method for reducing a large number of risk and protective factor measures to two derived indexes. However, there are also several limitations to this approach. First, such composite indexes hinder our ability to infer which specific risk or protective factors are contributing to the obtained relations with outcome variables (e.g., delay in alcohol initiation) and thus hamper our insight into explanatory mechanisms.

Second, risk and protective factors may include variables from different levels of analysis, for instance, school, family, peers, or temperament. When statistically significant findings are indicated for the risk or protective factor indexes, the preventive intervention implications may be difficult to infer because of unknown specificity with regard to the alternative levels incorporated in the composite index. In this situation, if school-level effects were dominant in the prediction of the outcome variable (e.g., alcohol initiation, level of alcohol use) rather than family-level effects, different preventive intervention implications would be inferred. Third, on a more technical note, composite indexes represented as latent variables (e.g., Jessor et al., 1995; Newcomb & Felix-Ortiz, 1992) assume unidimensionality and additivity with respect to the derived factors. In most instances, it is highly likely that both of these assumptions may be incorrect—these composite scores may be multidimensional, and the interrelations among individual risk and protective factor scores may be nonlinear (i.e., multiplicative interactions may exacerbate or attenuate relationships with outcome variables). Issues related to the scoring and statistical modeling and testing of multiple risk and multiple protective factors are important for the elaboration and usefulness of the approach to advance the field of adolescent alcohol use and other problem behaviors.

PREVENTION AND TREATMENT RESEARCH

Issues in Prevention Research

Prevention science represents an integration of disciplines (e.g., clinical and developmental psychology, education, public health) focused on (a) the identification and developmental course of risk and protective processes; (b) the evolving influences of risk and protective factors across the lifespan in relation to a variety of behaviors, such as alcohol and drug use, psychiatric disorders, and criminality; and (c) the incorporation of knowledge obtained about risk and protective factors to guide applied interventions (e.g., Coie et al., 1993; Bryant, West, & Windle, 1997). This emerging paradigm for prevention research thus links quite closely the notion of applied interventions within the context of ongoing person-environment confrontations with, and adaptations to, age-appropriate developmental tasks. The prevention science paradigm is likely to increase in prominence in the coming years and thus should facilitate the identification of future research directions.

Future research in the field of adolescent substance use prevention would be advanced by addressing several specific issues that are consistent with the prevention science paradigm. First, a number of prevention researchers have indicated a need for the development and evaluation of prevention programs based on the extant theoretical and empirical literature (e.g., Catalano et al., 1996; Gorman, 1996b; Spoth & Redmond, 1996). In this regard, Sussman, Petosa, and Clarke (1996) have advocated the empirical development of prevention curriculum, which they define as an evaluation of the intervention components as they are developed. Four steps in the empirical curriculum development process are (a) adopting and extending a theoretical knowledge base, (b) pooling curriculum activities, (c) testing individual activities, and (d) testing a full curriculum. According to Sussman et al. (1996), empirical curriculum development provides prevention researchers with a means of testing whether their theoretically based programs are operating in the ways they were hypothesized to operate. For example, are the variables that are the targets of intervention (e.g., changes in problem-solving skills) causally related to outcome behaviors as suggested by the intervention's theoretical framework? That is, do changes in hypothesized causal variables result in changes in outcome variables in the predicted directions?

Issues surrounding the need to investigate causal relations among intervention variables is an important feature of the prevention science approach (Coie et al., 1993; West & Aiken, 1997), with one of its aims being to adequately model the intervening processes that contribute to modifications in behavior. For example, West and Aiken (1997) state that many recent interventions consist of multicomponent programs (e.g., teen education, parent management-skills training, media messages) that target different response systems (for instance, more informed adolescent decision-making, less conflictual parent-adolescent relations) toward the same end state of the reduction of some risky behavior, such as alcohol use. If such multicomponent programs are successful in modifying alcohol use, the research question then becomes, which components were the most useful, and did they indeed affect the intended intervening variables in the manner hypothesized? This level of critical analysis is necessary for several reasons. First, it facilitates an evaluation of which components of an intervention are most effective in producing behavioral change and which ones are not; this is necessary for cost-benefit analyses to determine cost efficiency in intervention applications. Second, the study of the hypothesized mediating mechanisms, such as reduction in parent-adolescent conflict associated with parent skills training, facilitates the evaluation of why a given intervention component is or is not effective, as well as what other mediating mechanisms may be affected, either positively or negatively, by the component. For instance, better decision making by adolescents with regard to alcohol use may facilitate positive parent-adolescent communication. Third, the study of mediating mechanisms for preventive interventions enables systematic comparisons across groups (gender groups, age groups, racial-ethnic groups) to evaluate if the same or different mediational mechanisms exist across groups. Although this level of analysis is challenging, the field of adolescent alcohol use will benefit from such analyses.

A second area in need of additional focus in future research is the identification of the most effective strategies for identifying youth at high risk for the development of substance use and abuse and the development of interventions that most optimally facilitate positive change. For the Jump Start program, Harrington and Donohew (1997) based their identification of African American youths high on sensation-seeking characteristics on theoretical and empirical literature that suggested that high sensation seekers may be at especially high risk for the development of substance use problems. The development of the Jump Start program was tailored to meet the specific needs of these adolescents. Werch and DiClemente (1994) proposed the use of a multicomponent motivational stages (McMOS) conceptual model for the development of prevention programs targeted to adolescents at differing developmental stages of substance use acquisition. The McMOS model theorizes five stages of substance use acquisition: (a) precontemplation (not considering use), (b) contemplation (seriously thinking of initiating use), (c) preparation (intending to use in the near future), (d) action (initiating actual use), and (e) maintenance (continuing use). Werch and DiClemente propose a matching program strategy approach in which the content is tailored to the adolescents' specific developmental substance use acquisition stage.

A third area in need of subsequent research is the study of community-wide preventive interventions, especially in high-risk neighborhoods characterized by economic impoverishment, social dislocation, and high concentrations of inexpensive drugs (Aguirre-Molina & Gorman, 1996; Gorman & Speer, 1996). To be optimally effective, community programs must target multiple systems (family, media, local businesses, religious organizations, government, and law enforcement) and use multiple strategies, such as school-based curricula, partnerships between local businesses and schools that promote anti-substance-use messages and behaviors, and the formation of community task forces that work for macro-level political and legislative changes (Aguirre-Molina & Gorman, 1996; Williams et al., in press). In addition, essential to substance use prevention programs within economically and socially disadvantaged communities is the empowerment of residents via their integral involvement in problem identification and in the planning, development, and implementation of such programs (Aguirre-Molina & Gorman, 1996; Gorman & Speer, 1996). Engaging residents at this level of the prevention process is perhaps the greatest challenge facing community prevention researchers.

Issues in Treatment Research

A wide range of treatment approaches have been used with adolescent alcohol and drug abusers, including the 12-step model (e.g., Alcoholics Anonymous meetings), behavioral training (e.g., problem-solving skills, refusal skills), family therapy (e.g., parent management strategies), and educational and vocational assistance (Bukstein, 1994; Wheeler & Malmquist, 1987). Although some general guidelines have been proposed for the treatment of substance-abusing adolescents (e.g., Bukstein, 1994; Fleisch, 1991), critical reviews of this literature suggest that a number of methodological limitations, such as no control group, poor preassessment measures, poor follow-up, inadequate measures of treatment success or relapse, preclude more definitive answers to important questions. For example, few scientifically adequate comparative studies have been conducted to evaluate the efficacy of alternative treatment approaches with regard to short-term and long-term success or with regard to the generalizability of the substance intervention to other domains of functioning, for example, school or occupational adjustment, peer and family relations, or reduction in sexually risky behaviors. Furthermore, studies on the matching of adolescents with alcohol and drug disorders to alternative treatment approaches have not been evaluated for efficacy with regard to outcomes. Consequently, data are not readily available to guide critical decision making about what works best with whom.

The clinical ramifications of the high rates of multiple substance abuse (e.g., alcohol and cocaine) and of psychiatric comorbidity (i.e., a substance abuse disorder and a psychiatric disorder) among adolescents are numerous and have yet to be fully addressed in adolescent treatment settings or research applications (e.g., Bukstein et al., 1989). From the standpoint of etiology and treatment, it is important to investigate the relative ordering of onset (primary or secondary) for comorbid conditions and the implications of comorbidity itself for treatment responsivity, specificity of treatment (e.g., family therapy and pharmacotherapy), and relapse risk . Although alcohol-specific pharmaceutical agents, such as naltrexone, are not currently used with adolescents, if such agents are successful with adults, they may eventually be used (initially experimentally) with adolescents. Combination therapies (e.g., pharmacologic and psychosocial or behavioral) are commonly practiced with some psychiatric disorders, such as attention-deficit disorder. The comorbid conditions observed among adolescents in alcohol and drug treatment settings suggest that such combination approaches may be valuable additions (and treatment options) to tackle the multiple problems of highly troubled adolescents. Given the high rate of relapse among adolescents in substance abuse treatment settings (e.g., Brown et al., 1990), and the need to redirect these adolescents toward more constructive life course trajectories, greater knowledge of pharmacotherapy and combination therapies merits high priority in subsequent treatment research.

SUMMARY

This chapter identified several of the larger conceptual and methodological issues confronting the further study of adolescent alcohol use. Much of the early research on adolescent alcohol use was conducted by descriptive epidemiologists focused on issues such as the prevalence and correlates of adolescent alcohol use (with some notable exceptions such as Jessor & Jessor, 1977; Zucker et al., 1995). In this chapter, it was proposed that the current research agenda on adolescent alcohol use is focused much more on explanatory models to account for the cross-sectional and longitudinal variation observed with regard to adolescent drinking practices. A dynamic, contextual perspective, with an emphasis on adolescent development, was proposed as suitable for the objective of examining explanatory models and mechanisms. Such a model was deemed useful for more closely linking alcohol use with the ongoing adaptational tasks associated with adolescent development. The increased use of prospective, multiple-mediator models to test hypothesized relations among variables was also suggested.

Several conceptual and methodological issues in risk and protective factors research were also identified. These included conceptual issues about main and interaction effects models; the need to recognize the bidirectional relations between risk and protective factors and problem behaviors, such as alcohol initiation and alcohol use; and scoring issues for composite indexes of risk and protectiveness. Each of these issues needs to be carefully addressed in future research to increase the contribution of this framework to the field. Last, several issues related to prevention and treatment research were provided. Similar to some of the issues discussed with regard to conceptual models of adolescent alcohol use, there is a need for more refined hypothesis testing about preventive interventions and their presumed effects. The clinical implications of comorbidity among adolescents in treatment settings was briefly discussed, along with suggestions for increased research on comparative treatment efficacy. It may be concluded that the research agenda is fertile for the study of adolescent alcohol use and abuse. Addressing the multiple concerns that have arisen with regard to adolescent alcohol use provides researchers and health care providers with major challenges for subsequent research and application.

REFERENCES

Adler, I., & Kandel, D. B. (1983). Risk periods for drug involvement in adolescence in France and in Israel: Application of survival analysis to cross-sectional data. *Social Forces, 62,* 375-394.

Aguirre-Molina, M., & Gorman, D. M. (1996). Community-based approaches for the prevention of alcohol, tobacco, and other drug use. *Annual Review of Public Health, 17,* 337-358.

Alterman, A. I., O'Brien, C. P., & McLellan, A. J. (1991). Differential therapeutics for substance abuse. In R. J. Frances & S. I. Miller (Eds.), *Clinical textbook of addictive disorders* (pp. 369-390). New York: Guilford.

American Psychiatric Association. (1987). *Diagnostic and statistical manual of mental disorders* (3rd ed., rev.). Washington, DC: Author.

American Psychiatric Association. (1994). *Diagnostic and statistical manual of mental disorders* (4th ed.). Washington, DC: Author.

American School Health Association, Association for the Advancement of Health Education, and Society for Public Health Education, Inc. (1989). *The National Adolescent Student Health Survey: A report on the health of America's youth.* Oakland, CA: Third Party Publishing.

Arnett, T. (1992). Reckless behavior in adolescence: A developmental perspective. *Developmental Review, 12,* 339-373.

Ary, D. V., Tildesley, E., Hops, H., & Andrews, J. (1993). The influence of parent, sibling, and peer modeling and attitudes on adolescent use of alcohol. *The International Journal of the Addictions, 28,* 853-880.

August, G. J., Stewart, M. A., & Holmes, C. S. (1983). A four-year follow-up of hyperactive boys with and without conduct disorder. *British Journal of Psychiatry, 143,* 192-198.

Bachman, J. G., Wallace, J., Jr., O'Malley, P. M., Johnston, L. D., Kurth, C. L., & Neighbors, M. W. (1991). Racial/ethnic differences in smoking, drinking and illicit drug use among American high school seniors, 1976-1989. *American Journal of Public Health, 81,* 372-377.

Bahr, S. J., Hawks, R. D., & Wang, G. (1993). Family and religious influences on adolescent substance abuse. *Youth & Society, 24,* 443-465.

Bailey, S. L., Flewelling, R. L., & Rachal, J. V. (1992). The characterization of inconsistencies in self-reports of alcohol and marijuana use in longitudinal study of adolescents. *Journal of Studies on Alcohol, 53,* 636-647.

Bailey, S. L., & Rachal, J. V. (1993). Dimensions of adolescent problem drinking. *Journal of Studies on Alcohol, 54,* 555-565.

Barnes, G. M. (1990). Impact of the family on adolescent drinking patterns. In R. L. Collins, K. E. Leonard, and J. S. Searles (Eds.), *Alcohol and the family: Research and clinical perspectives* (pp. 137-161). New York: Guilford.

Barnes, G. M., & Welte, J. W. (1986). Patterns and predictors of alcohol use among 7-12th grade students in New York State. *Journal of Studies on Alcohol, 47,* 53-62.

Baron, R. M., & Kenny, D. A. (1986). The moderator-mediator variable distinction in social psychological research: Conceptual, strategic, and statistical considerations. *Journal of Personality and Social Psychology, 57,* 1173-1182.

Bauman, K. E., & Ennett, S. T. (1996). On the importance of peer influence for adolescent drug use: Commonly neglected considerations. *Addiction, 91,* 185.

Bauman, K. E., Fisher, L. A., Bryan, E. E. S., & Chenowith, R. L. (1985). Relationships between subjective expected utility and behavior: A longitudinal study of adolescent drinking behavior. *Journal of Studies on Alcohol, 46,* 32-38.

Baumrind, D., & Moselle, K. A. (1985). A developmental perspective on adolescent drug abuse. *Alcohol and Substance Abuse in Adolescence, 2,* 41-67.

Bettes, B. A., Dusenbury, L., Kerner, J., James-Ortiz, S., & Botvin, G. J. (1990). Ethnicity and psychosocial factors in alcohol and tobacco use in adolescence. *Child Development, 61,* 557-565.

Biderman, J. (1992). New developments in pediatric psychopharmacology. *Journal of the American Academy of Child and Adolescent Psychiatry, 31,* 14-15.

Blackson, T. C., Tarter, R. E., Loeber, R., Ammerman, R. T., & Windle, M. (1996). The influence of paternal substance abuse and difficult temperament in fathers and sons on son's disengagement from family to deviant peers. *Journal of Youth and Adolescence, 25,* 389-411.

Blouin, A. G. A., Bornstein, R. A., & Trites, R. L. (1978). Teenage alcohol use among hyperactive children: A five-year follow-up study. *Journal of Pediatric Psychiatry, 116,* 188-194.

Blum, K., Noble, E. P., Sheridan, P. J., Montgomery, A., Ritchie, T., Jagadeeswaran, P., Nogam, H., Briggs, A. H., & Cohen, J. B. (1990). Allelic associations of human dopamine D2 receptor gene and alcoholism. *Journal of the American Medical Association, 263,* 2055-2060.

Botvin, G. J., Baker, E., Dusenbury, L., Botvin, E. M., & Diaz, T. (1995). Long-term follow-up results of a randomized drug abuse prevention trial in a white middle-class population. *Journal of the American Medical Association, 273,* 1106-1112.

Botvin, G. J., Baker, E., Dusenbury, L., Tortu, S., & Botvin, E. M. (1990). Preventing adolescent drug abuse through a multimodal cognitive-behavioral approach: Results of a 3-year study. *Journal of Consulting and Clinical Psychology, 58,* 437-446.

Brook, J. S., Brook, D. W., Gordon, A. S., Whiteman, M., & Cohen, P. (1990). The psychosocial etiology of adolescent drug use: A family interactional approach. *Genetic, Social and General Psychology Monographs, 116,* 111-267.

Brown, S. (1993). Recovery patterns in adolescent substance abuse. In J. S. Baer, G. A. Marlott, & R. J. McMahon (Eds.), *Addictive behaviors across the life span: Prevention, treatment, and policy issue* (pp. 161-183). Newbury Park, CA: Sage.

Brown, S. A., Gleghorn, A., Schuckit, M. A., Myers, M. G., & Mott, M. A. (1996). Conduct disorder among adolescent alcohol and drug abusers. *Journal of Studies on Alcohol, 57,* 314-324.

Brown, S. A., Mott, M. A., & Myers, M. G. (1990). Adolescent alcohol and drug treatment outcome. In R. R.Watson (Ed.), *Drug and alcohol abuse prevention* (pp. 373-403). Clifton, NJ: Humana.

Brown, S. A., Vik, P. W., & Creamer, V. A. (1989). Characteristics of relapse following adolescent substance abuse treatment. *Addictive Behaviors, 14,* 291-300.

Bryant, K. J., West, S. G., & Windle, M. (1997). Overview of new methodological developments in prevention research: Alcohol and substance abuse. In K. J. Bryant, M. Windle, & S. G. West (Eds.), *The science of prevention: Methodological advances from alcohol and substance abuse research* (pp. xvii-xxxii). Washington, DC: American Psychological Association.

Bryk, A. S., & Raudenbush, S. W. (1992). *Hierarchical linear and nonlinear modeling with the HLM/2L and HLM/3L programs.* Chicago: Scientific Software International.

Bukstein, O., & Kaminer, Y. (1994). The nosology of adolescent substance abuse. *American Journal of Addictions, 3,* 1-13.

Bukstein, O. G. (1994). Treatment of adolescent alcohol abuse and dependence. *Alcohol Health and Research World, 18,* 196-301.

Bukstein, O. G., Brent, D. A., & Kaminer, Y. (1989). Comorbidity of substance use and other psychiatric disorders in adolescents. *American Journal of Psychiatry, 146,* 1131-1141.

Buydens-Branchey, L., Branchey, M. H., Noumair, D., & Lieber, C. S. (1989). Age of alcoholism onset. *Archives of General Psychiatry, 46,* 231-236.

Campanelli, P. C., Dielman, T. E., & Shope, J. T. (1987). Validity of adolescents' self-reports of alcohol use and misuse using a bogus pipeline procedure. *Adolescence, 22,* 7-22.

Catalano, R. F., Hawkins, J. D., Wells, E. A., Miller, J., & Brewer, D. D. (1991). Evaluation of the effectiveness of adolescent drug abuse treatment, assessment of risks for relapse, and promising approaches for relapse prevention. *International Journal of the Addictions, 25,* 1085-1140.

Catalano, R. F., Kosterman, R., Hawkins, J. D., Newcomb, M. D., & Abbott, R. D. (1996). Modeling the etiology of adolescent substance use: A test of the social development model. *Journal of Drug Issues, 26,* 429-455.

Chassin, L., Pillow, D. R., Curran, P. J., Molina, B. S. G., & Barrera, M. (1993). Relation of parental alcoholism to early adolescent substance use: A test of three mediating mechanisms. *Journal of Abnormal Psychology, 102,* 3-19.

Christiansen, B. A., & Teahan, J. E. (1987). Cross-cultural comparisons of Irish and American adolescent drinking practices and beliefs. *Journal of Studies on Alcohol, 48,* 558-562.

Christiansen, B. A., Goldman, M. S., & Inn, A. (1982). Development of alcohol-related expectancies in adolescents: Separating pharmacological from social-learning influences. *Journal of Consulting and Clinical Psychology, 50,* 336-344.

Christiansen, B. A., Smith, G. T., Roehling, P. V., & Goldman, M. S. (1989). Using alcohol expectancies to predict adolescent drinking behavior after one year. *Journal of Consulting and Clinical Psychology, 57,* 93-99.

Clark, D. B., Jacob, R. G., & Mezzich, A. (1994). Anxiety and conduct disorders in early onset alcoholism. In T. F. Babor, V. Hesselbrock, R. Meyer, & W. Shoemaker (Eds.), *Types of alcoholics* (pp. 181-186). New York: New York Academy of Sciences.

Cloninger, C. R., Sigvardsson, S., & Bohman, M. (1988). Childhood personality predicts alcohol abuse in young adults. *Alcoholism: Clinical and Experimental Research, 12,* 494-504.

Cloninger, C. R., Bohman, M., & Sigvardsson, S. (1981). Inheritance of alcohol abuse: Cross-fostering analysis of adopted men. *Archives of General Psychiatry, 38,* 861-868.

Coate, D., & Grossman, M. (1988). Effects of alcoholic beverage prices and legal drinking ages on youth alcohol use. *Journal of Law & Economics, 31,* 145-171.

Cohen, P., Cohen, J., Kasen, S., Velez, C. N., Hartmark, C., Johnson, J., Rojas, M., Brook, J., & Streuning, E. L. (1993). An epidemiological study of disorders in late childhood and adolescence: I. Age- and gender-specific prevalence. *Journal of Child Psychology and Psychiatry, 34,* 851-867.

Coie, J. D., Watt, N. F., West, S. G., Hawkins, J. D., Asarnow, J. R., Markman, H. J., Ramey, S. L., Shure, M. B., & Long, B. (1993). The science of prevention: A conceptual framework and some directions for a national research program. *American Psychologist, 48,* 1013-1022.

Cooper, M. L. (1994). Motivations for alcohol use among adolescents: Development and validation of a four-factor model. *Psychological Assessment, 6,* 117-128.

Cooper, M. L., Russell, M., & George, W. H. (1988). Coping, expectancies, and alcohol abuse: A test of social learning formulations. *Journal of Abnormal Psychology, 97,* 218-230.

Dawson, D. A. (1998). Volume of ethanol consumption: Effects of different approaches to measurement. *Journal of Studies on Alcohol, 59,* 191-197.

Deckel, A. W., Hesselbrock, V., & Bauer, L. (1995). Relationship between alcohol-related expectancies and anterior brain functioning in young men at risk for developing alcoholism. *Alcoholism: Clinical & Experimental Research, 19,* 476-481.

Dielman, T. E., Shope, J. T., Butchart, A. T., & Campanelli, P. C. (1986). Prevention of adolescent alcohol misuse: An elementary school program. *Journal of Pediatric Psychology, 1,* 259-282.

Dielman, T. E., Shope, J. T., Leech, S. L., & Butchart, A. T. (1989). Differential effectiveness of an elementary school-based alcohol misuse prevention program. *Journal of School Health, 59,* 255-263.

Dishion, T. J., Andrews, D. W., Kavanaugh, K., & Soberman, L. H. (1996). Preventive interventions for high-risk youth: The Adolescent Transitions Program. In R. D. Peters & R. J. McMahon (Eds.), *Preventing childhood disorders, substance abuse, and delinquency* (pp. 184-214). Thousand Oaks, CA: Sage.

Dobkin, P. L., Tremblay, R. E., Masse, L. C., & Vitaro, F. (1995). Individual and peer characteristics in predicting boys' early onset of substance abuse: A seven-year longitudinal study. *Child Development, 66,* 1198-1214.

Donovan, J. E., & Jessor, R. (1978). Adolescent problem drinking: Psychosocial correlates in a national sample study. *Journal of Studies on Alcohol, 39,* 1506-1524.

Duncan, T.E., Tildesley, E., Duncan, S. C., & Hops, H. (1995). The consistency of family and peer influences on the development of substance use in adolescence. *Addiction, 90,* 1647-1660.

Ellickson, P. L., & Bell, R. M. (1990). Drug prevention in junior high: A multi-site longitudinal test. *Science, 247,* 1299-1304.

Ellickson, P. L., Bell, R. M., & McGuigan, K. (1993). Preventing adolescent drug use: Long-term results of a junior high program. *American Journal of Public Health, 83,* 856-861.

Elliott, D. S., Huizinga, D., & Menard, S. (1989). *Multiple problem youth.* New York: Springer-Verlag.

Erikson, E. H. (1963). *Childhood and society.* New York: Norton.

Fingarette, H. (1989). *Heavy drinking: The myth of alcoholism as a disease.* Berkeley: University of California Press.

Fleisch, B. (1991). *Approaches in the treatment of adolescents with emotional and substance abuse problems.* Rockville, MD: U.S. Department of Health and Human Services.

Garmezy, N., & Rutter, M. (Eds.). (1983). *Stress, coping and development in children.* New York: McGraw-Hill.

Giancola, P. R., & Zeichner, A. (1997). The biphasic effects of alcohol on human physical aggression. *Journal of Abnormal Psychology, 106,* 598-607.

Gillmore, M. R., Hawkins, J. D., Catalano, R. F., Day, L. E., & Moore, M. (1991). Structure of problem behavior in preadolescence. *Journal of Consulting and Clinical Psychology, 59,* 499-506.

Goldstein, H. (1995). *Multilevel statistical models* (2nd ed.). London: Edward Arnold.

Gorman, D. M. (1992). Using theory and basic research to target primary prevention programs: Recent developments and future prospects. *Alcohol & Alcoholism, 27,* 583-594.

Gorman, D. M. (1995). Are school-based resistance skills training programs effective in preventing alcohol misuse? *Journal of Alcohol and Drug Education, 41,* 74-98.

Gorman, D. M. (1996a). Do school-based social skills training programs prevent alcohol use among young people? *Addiction Research, 4,* 191-210.

Gorman, D. M. (1996b). Etiological theories and the primary prevention of drug use. *Journal of Drug Issues, 26,* 505-520.

Gorman, D. M. (1998). The irrelevance of evidence in the development of school-based drug prevention policy, 1986-1996. *Evaluation Review, 22,* 118-146.

Gorman, D. M., & Speer, P. W. (1996). Preventing alcohol abuse and alcohol-related problems through community interventions: A review of evaluation studies. *Psychology and Health, 11,* 95-131.

Grant, B., & Dawson, D. A. (1998). Age of alcohol onset and alcohol disorders. *Journal of Substance Abuse.*

Grossman, M., Coate, D., & Arluck, G. M. (1987). Price sensitivity of alcoholic beverages in the United States: Youth alcohol consumption. In H. Holder (Ed.), *Control issues in alcohol abuse prevention: Strategies for states and communities* (pp. 169-198). Greenwich, CT: JAI.

Gruenewald, P. J., Miller, A. B., Treno, A. J., Yang, Z., Ponicki, W. R., & Roeper, P. (1996). The geography of availability and driving after drinking. *Addiction, 91,* 967-983.

Harrell, A. V., Sowder, B., & Kapsak, K. (1988). *Field Validation of Drinking and You: A screening instrument for adolescent problem drinking* (Contract No. ADM 281-85-0007). Rockville, MD: National Institute of Alcohol Abuse and Alcoholism.

Harrell, A. V., & Wirtz, P. W. (1989). Screening for adolescent problem drinking: Validation of a multidimensional instrument for case identification. *Psychological Assessment, 1,* 61-63.

Harrington, N. G., & Donohew, L. (1997). Jump Start: A targeted substance abuse prevention program. *Health Education & Behavior, 24,* 568-586.

Hawkins, J. D., Catalano, R. F., & Miller, J. Y. (1992). Risk and protective factors for alcohol and other drug problems in adolescence and early adulthood: Implications for substance abuse prevention. *Psychological Bulletin, 112,* 64-105.

Haynes, S. N. (1992). *Models of causality in psychopathology: Toward dynamic, synthetic, and nonlinear causal models of behavior disorders.* New York: Macmillan.

Heath, A. C. (1995). Genetic influences on drinking behavior in humans. In H. Begleiter & B. Kissin (Eds.), *Alcohol and alcoholism: Vol. 1. The genetic factors and alcoholism.* Oxford, UK: Oxford University Press.

Heath, A. C., Sluske, W. S., & Madden, P. A. F. (1997). Gender differences in the genetic contribution to alcoholism risk and to alcohol consumption patterns. In R. W. Wilsnack & S. C. Wilsnack (Eds.), *Gender and alcohol* (pp. 114-149). Rutgers, NJ: Rutgers University Press.

Helzer, J., Canino, G., & Yeh, E. K. (1990). Alcoholism—North America and Asia. *Archives of General Psychiatry, 47,* 313-319.

Helzer, J. E., & Pryzbeck, T. R. (1988). The co-occurrence of alcoholism with other psychiatric disorders in the general population and its impact on treatment. *Journal of Studies on Alcohol, 49,* 219-224.

Henly, G. A., & Winters, K. C. (1989). Development of psychosocial scales for the assessment of adolescents involved in alcohol and drugs. *International Journal of Addictions, 24,* 973-1001.

Hingson, R., Heeren, T., & Winter, M. (1994). Effects of lower legal blood alcohol limits for young and adult drivers. *Alcohol, Drugs and Driving, 10,* 243-251.

Hingson, R., Heeren, T., & Winter, M. (1996). Lowering state legal blood alcohol limits to 0.08%: The effect on fatal motor vehicle crashes. *American Journal of Public Health, 86,* 1297-1299.

Holly, A., & Wittchen, H. U. (1998). Patterns of use and their relationship to DSM-IV abuse and dependence of alcohol among adolescents and young adults. *European Addiction Research, 4,* 50-57.

Hops, H., Tildesley, E., Lichtenstein, E., Ary, D., & Sherman, L. (1990). Parent-adolescent problem-solving interactions and drug use. *American Journal of Drug and Alcohol Abuse, 16,* 239-258.

Huba, G. J., & Bentler, P. B. (1982). A developmental theory of drug use: Derivation and assessment of a causal modeling approach. In P. B. Baltes & O. G. Brim, Jr. (Eds.), *Life Span Development and Behavior* (Vol. 4; pp. 147-203). New York: Academic Press.

Ingvar, M., Ghatan, P. H., Wirsen-Meurling, A., Risberg, J., Von Heijne, G., Stone-Elander, S., & Ingvar, D. M. (1998). Alcohol activates the cerebral reward system in man. *Journal of Studies on Alcohol, 59,* 258-269.

Institute of Medicine. (1994). *Reducing risks for mental disorders: Frontiers for preventive intervention research.* Washington, DC: National Academy Press.

Jacob, T., & Leonard, K. (1994). Family and peer influences in the development of adolescent alcohol abuse. In R. Rucker & J. Howard (Eds.), *Development of alcohol problems: Exploring the biopsychosocial matrix of risk* (pp. 123-155; NIAA Research Monograph No. 26, NIH Publication No. 94-3495). Rockville, MD: National Institutes for Health.

Jessor, R., Donovan, J. E., & Costa, F. N. (1991). *Beyond adolescence: Problem behavior and young adult development.* Cambridge, MA: Cambridge University Press.

Jessor, R., & Jessor, S. L. (1977). *Problem behavior and psychosocial development: A longitudinal study of youth.* New York: Academic Press.

Jessor, R., Van Den Bos, J., Vanderryn, J., Costa, F. M., & Turbin, M. S. (1995). Protective factors in adolescent problem behavior: Moderator effects and developmental change. *Developmental Psychology, 31,* 923-933.

Johnson, C. A., Pentz, M. A., Weber, M. D., Dwyer, J. H., Baer, N., MacKinnon, D. P., Hansen, W. B., & Flay, B. R. (1990). Relative effectiveness of comprehensive community programming for drug abuse prevention with high-risk and low-risk adolescents. *Journal of Consulting and Clinical Psychology, 58,* 447-456.

Johnson, E. O., Arria, A. M., Borges, G., Ialongo, N., & Anthony, J. C. (1995). The growth of conduct problem behaviors from middle childhood to early adolescence: Sex differences and the suspected influence of early alcohol use. *Journal of Studies on Alcohol, 56,* 661-671.

Johnston, L. D., O'Malley, P. M., & Bachman, J. G. (1991). *Drug use among American high school students, college students, and other young adults, 1975-1990.* Rockville, MA: National Institute on Drug Abuse.

Johnston, L. D., O'Malley, P. M., & Bachman, J. G. (1996). *National survey results on drug use from the Monitoring the Future Study, 1975-1994: Vol. 1. Secondary school students.* Rockville, MD: National Institute on Drug Abuse.

Kaminer, Y. (1995). Pharmacotherapy for adolescents with psychoactive substance abuse disorders. In E. Rahdert & D. Czechowicz (Eds.), *Adolescent drug abuse: Clinical assessment and therapeutic interventions* (pp. 291-324; NIDA Research Monograph 156, NIH Publication No. 95-3908). Washington, DC: U.S. Department of Health and Human Services.

Kaminer, Y., Tarter, R. E., Bukstein, O. G., & Kabene, M. (1992). Comparison between treatment completers and noncompleters among dually diagnosed substance-abusing adolescents. *Journal of the American Academy of Child & Adolescent Psychiatry, 31,* 1046-1049.

Kandel, D. B. (1975). Stages in adolescent involvement in drug use. *Science, 181,* 912-914.

Kandel, D. B. (1980). Drug and drinking behavior among youth. *Annual Review in Sociology, 6,* 235-285.

Kandel, D. B. (1985). On processes of peer influences in adolescent drug use: A developmental perspective. *Advances in Alcohol and Substance Abuse, 4,* 139-163.

Kashani, J. M., Beck, N. C., Hoeper, E. W., Fallahi, C., Corcoran, C. M., McAllister, J. A., Rosenberg, T. K., & Reid, C. (1987). Psychiatric disorders in a community sample of adolescents. *American Journal of Psychiatry, 148,* 564-589.

Kendler, K. S., Heath, A. S., Neale, M. C., Kessler, R. C., & Eaves, L. J. (1992). A population based twin study of alcoholism in women. *Journal of the American Medical Association, 268,* 1877-1882.

Kohnstamm, G. A., Bates, J. E., & Rothbart, M. K. (Eds.). (1989). *Temperament in childhood.* New York: John Wiley.

Koob, G. F., & Bloom, F. E. (1988). Cellular and molecular mechanisms of drug dependence. *Science, 242,* 715-723.

Kumar, K. M., & O'Brien, C. P. (1994). Substance abuse. In A. Frazier, P. Molinoff, & A. Winokur (Eds.), *Biological bases of brain function and disease* (pp. 357-384). New York: Raven.

Kumpfer, K. L., Molgaard, V., & Spoth, R. (1996). The Strengthening Families Program for the prevention of delinquency and drug use. In R. D. Peters & R. J. McMahon (Eds.), *Preventing childhood disorders, substance abuse, and delinquency* (pp. 241-267). Thousand Oaks, CA: Sage.

Labouvie, E. W. (1986). Alcohol and marijuana use in relation to adolescent stress. *International Journal of Addictions, 21,* 333-345.

Lazarus, R. S., & Folkman, S. (1984). *Stress, appraisal, and coping.* New York: Springer.

Leccese, M., & Waldron, H. B. (1994). Assessing adolescent substance use: A critique of current measurement instruments. *Journal of Substance Abuse Treatment, 11,* 553-563.

Lemmens, P., Tan, E. S., & Knibbe, R. A.(1992). Measuring quantity and frequency of drinking in a general population survey: A comparison of five indices. *Journal of Studies on Alcohol, 53,* 476-486.

Loeber, R., Farrington, D. P., Stouthamer-Loeber, & Van Kammen, W. B. (1998). *Antisocial behavior and mental health problems: Explanatory factors in childhood and adolescence.* Mahwah, NJ: Erlbaum.

Lerner, J. V., & Lerner, R. M. (1983). Temperament and adaptation across life: Theoretical and empirical issues. In P. B. Baltes & O. G. Brim, Jr. (Eds.), *Life span development and behavior* (Vol. 5; pp 197-231). New York: Academic Press.

Maddahian, E., Newcomb, M. D., & Bentler, P. M. (1988). Risk factors for substance use: Ethnic differences among adolescents. *Journal of Substance Abuse, 1,* 11-23.

Magnusson, D. (1988). *Individual development from an interactional perspective: A longitudinal study.* Hillsdale, NJ: Erlbaum.

Mann, L. M., Chassin, L., & Sher, K. J. (1987). Alcohol expectancies and the risk for alcoholism. *Journal of Consulting and Clinical Psychology, 55,* 411-417.

Martin, C., Earlywine, M., Musty, R., Perrine, M., & Swift, R. (1993). Development and validation of the biphasic alcohol effects scale. *Alcoholism: Clinical and Experimental Research, 17,* 140-146.

Martin, C. S., Kaczynski, N. A., Maisto, S. A., Bukstein, O. M., & Moss, H. B. (1995). Patterns of DSM-IV alcohol abuse and dependence symptoms in adolescent drinkers. *Journal of Studies on Alcohol, 56,* 672-680.

McCord, W., & McCord, J. (1960). *Origins of alcoholism.* Stanford, CA: Stanford University Press.

McGee, L., & Newcomb, M. D. (1992). General deviance syndrome: Expanded hierarchical evaluations at four ages from early adolescence to adulthood. *Journal of Consulting and Clinical Psychology, 60,* 766-776.

McGue, M. (1994). Genes, environment and the etiology of alcoholism. In R. Zucker, G. Boyd, and J. Howard (Eds.), *Development of alcohol-related problems: Exploring the biopsychosocial matrix of risk* (pp. 1-40; National Institute on Alcoholism and Alcohol Abuse Research Monograph No. 26). Rockville, MD: National Institute on Alcoholism and Alcohol Abuse.

McGue, M. (1995). Mediators and moderators of alcoholism inheritance. In J. R. Turner, L. R. Cardon, & J. K. Hewitt (Eds.), *Behavior genetic approaches in behavioral medicine* (pp. 17-44). New York: Plenum.

McGue, M., Sharma, A., & Benson, P. (1996). Parent and sibling influences on adolescent alcohol use and misuse: Evidence from a U.S. adoption cohort. *Journal of Studies on Alcohol, 57,* 8-18.

McLellan, A. T., Arndt, I. O., Metzger, D. S., Woody, G. E., & O'Brien, C. P. (1993). The effects of psychosocial services in substance abuse treatment. *Journal of the American Medical Association, 269,* 1953-1959.

McLellan, T., & Dembo, R. (1993). *Screening and assessment of alcohol- and other drug-abusing adolescents* (DHHS Publication No. SMA 93-2009). Washington, DC: U.S. Department of Health and Human Services, Center for Substance Abuse Treatment.

Mosher, J. F. (1980). The history of youthful-drinking laws: Implications for current policy. In H. Wechsler (Ed.), *Minimum drinking-age laws* (pp. 11-38). Lexington, MA: Lexington Books.

Myers, M. G., & Brown, S. A. (1990). Coping responses and relapse among adolescent substance abusers. *Journal of Substance Abuse, 2,* 177-189.

National Institute on Drug Abuse. (1985). *Self-report methods of estimating drug use: Meeting current challenges to validity* (NIDA Research Monograph No. 57; DHHS Publication No. ADM 85-1402). Washington, DC: Government Printing Office.

National Institute on Drug Abuse. (1994). *Assessing drug abuse among adolescents and adults: Standardized instruments* (NIH Publication No. 94-3757). Rockville, MD: Author.

Needle, R., McCubbin, H., Reineck, R., Lazar, A., & Mederer, H. (1986). Interpersonal influences in adolescent drug use—The role of older siblings, parents, and peers. *The International Journal of the Addictions, 21,* 739-766.

Newcomb, M. D., & Felix-Ortiz, M. (1992). Multiple protective and risk factors for drug use and abuse: Cross-sectional and prospective findings. *Journal of Personality and Social Psychology, 63,* 280-296.

Newcomb, M.D., Huba, G. J., & Bentler, P. M. (1981). A multidimensional assessment of stressful life events among adolescents: Derivation and correlates. *Journal of Health and Social Behavior, 22,* 400-415.

Noble, E. P. (1998). The D2 dopamine receptor gene: A review of association studies in alcoholism and phenotypes. *Alcohol, 16,* 33-45.

Norman, E., & Turner, S. (1993). Adolescent substance abuse prevention programs: Theories, models, and research in the encouraging 80's. *The Journal of Primary Prevention, 14,* 3-20.

O'Malley, P. M., & Wagenaar, A. C. (1991). Effects of minimum drinking age laws on alcohol use, related behaviors and traffic crash involvement among American youth: 1976-1987. *Journal of Studies on Alcohol, 52,* 478-491.

Oetting, E. R., & Beauvais, F. (1986). Peer cluster theory: Drugs and the adolescent. *Journal of Counseling and Development, 65,* 17-22.

Oetting, E. R., & Beauvais, F. (1990). Adolescent drug use: Findings of national and local surveys. *Journal of Consulting and Clinical Psychology, 58,* 382-394.

Office of National Drug Control Policy: The National Drug Control Strategy: 197 [On-line]. Available: *http://www.ncjrs.org/htm/chapter2.htm:* 1997.

Osgood, D. W., Johnston, L. D., O'Malley, P. M., & Bachman, J. G. (1988). The generality of deviance in late adolescent and early adulthood. *American Sociological Review, 53,* 81-93.

Pagliaro, A. M., & Pagliaro, L. A. (1996). *Substance use among children and adolescents.* New York: John Wiley.

Parsian, A., Todd, R. D., Devor, E. J., O'Malley, K. L., Suarez, B. K., Reich, T., & Cloninger, C. R. (1991). Alcoholism and alleles of the human D2 dopamine receptor locus: Studies of association and linkage. *Archives of General Psychiatry, 48,* 655-663.

Patterson, G. R. (1982). *Antisocial children, coercive family process.* Eugene, OR: Castalia.

Pentz, M. A., Dwyer, J. H., MacKinnon, D. P., Flay, B. R., Hansen, W. B., Wang, E. Y., & Johnson, C. A. (1989). A multicommunity trial for primary prevention of adolescent abuse. *Journal of the American Medical Association, 261,* 3259-3266.

Perry, C. L., Williams, C. L., Veblen-Mortenson, S., Toomey, T. L., Komro, K. A., Anstine, P. S., McGovern, P. G., Finnegan, J. R., Forster, J. L., Wagenaar, A. C., & Wolfson, M. (1996). Project Northland: Outcomes of a communitywide alcohol use prevention pro- gram dur- ing early adolescence. *American Journal of Public Health, 86,* 956-965.

Petraitis, J., Flay, B. R., & Miller, T. Q. (1995). Reviewing theories of adolescent substance use: Organizing pieces in the puzzle. *Psychological Bulletin, 117,* 67-86.

Plomin, R., DeFries, J. C., & McClearn, G. E. (1990). *Behavioral genetics: A primer* (2nd ed.) New York: Freeman.

Puig-Antich, J., & Chambers, W. (1978). *The schedule for affective disorders and schizophrenia for school-aged children.* New York: New York State Psychiatric Institute.

Rachal, J. V., Hubbard, R. L., Williams, J. R., & Tuchfeld, B. S. (1976). Drinking levels and problem drinking among junior and senior high school students. *Journal of Studies on Alcohol, 37,* 1751-1761.

Rahdert, E. R. (1991). *The adolescent assessment/referral system manual* (DHHS Publication No. ADM 91-1735). Rockville, MD: U.S. Department of Health and Human Services, Alcohol, Drug Abuse, and Mental Health Administration, National Institute on Drug Abuse.

Reed, M. D., & Rountree, P. W. (1997). Peer pressure and adolescent substance use. *Journal of Quantitative Criminology, 13,* 143-180.

Reese, F. L., Chassin, L., & Molina, B. S. G. (1994). Alcohol expectancies in early adolescents: Predicting drinking behavior from alcohol expectancies and parental alcoholism. *Journal of Studies on Alcohol, 55,* 276-284.

Reich, T., Edenberg, H. J., Goate, A., Williams, J. T., Rice, J. P., Rice, J. P., Van Eerdewegh, P., Foround, T., Hessselbrock, V., Schuckit, M. A., Bucholz, K., Porjesz, B., Li, T. K., Conneally, P. M., Nurnberger, Jr., J. I., Tischfield, J. A., Crowe, R. R., Cloninger, C. R., Wu, W., Shear, S., Carr, K., Crose, C., Willig, C., & Begleiter, H. (1998). Genome-wide search for genes affecting the risk for alcohol dependence. *American Journal of Medical Genetics, 81,* 207-215.

Reinherz, H. Z., Giaconia, R. M., Lefkowitz, E. S., Pakiz, B., & Frost, A. K. (1993). Prevalence of psychiatric disorders in a community population of older adolescents. *Journal of the American Academy of Child and Adolescent Psychiatry, 32,* 369-377.

Rhodes, J. E., Gingiss, P. L., & Smith, P. B. (1994). Risk and protective factors for alcohol use among pregnant African-American, Hispanic, and white adolescents: The influence of peers, sexual partners, family members, and mentors. *Addictive Behaviors, 19,* 555-564.

Robins, C. N. (1966). *Deviant children grown up.* Baltimore: Williams & Wilkins.

Rorabaugh, W. (1979). *The alcoholic republic: An American tradition.* New York: Oxford University Press.

Russell, M. (1990). Prevalence of alcoholism among children of alcoholics. In M. Windle & J.S. Searles (Eds.), *Children of alcoholics: Critical perspectives* (pp. 9-38). New York: Guilford.

Rutter, M. (1987). Psychosocial resilience and protective mechanisms. *American Journal of Orthopsychiatry, 57,* 316-333.

Sadava, S. W. (1985). Problem behavior theory and consumption and consequences of alcohol. *Journal of Studies on Alcohol, 46,* 392-397.

Saffer, H., & Grossman, M. (1987). Beer taxes, the legal drinking age, and youth motor vehicle fatalities. *Journal of Legal Studies, 16,* 351-374.

Schulenberg, J., Maggs, J. L., & Hurrelmann, K. (1997). *Health risks and developmental transitions during adolescence.* New York: Cambridge University Press.

Schulenberg, J., Wadsworth, K. N., O'Malley, P. M., Bachman, J. G., & Johnston, L. D. (1996). Adolescent risk factors for binge drinking during the transition to young adulthood: Variable- and pattern-centered approaches to change. *Developmental Psychology, 32,* 659-674.

Seilhamer, R. A., & Jacob, T. (1990). Family factors and adjustment of children of alcoholics. In M. Windle & J. S. Searles (Eds.), *Children of alcoholics: Critical perspectives* (pp. 168-186). New York: Guilford.

Sher, K. J. (Ed.). (1991). *Children of alcoholics: A critical appraisal of theory and research.* Chicago: University of Chicago Press.

Sher, K. J. (1994). Individual level risk factors. In R. A. Zucker, G. M. Boyd, & J. Howard (Eds.), *The development of alcohol problems: Exploring the biopsychosocial matrix of risk* (pp.77-121; NIAAA Monograph 26, NIH Publication No. 94-3495). Washington, DC: National Institutes of Health.

Shope, J. T., Dielman, T. E., Butchart, A. T., Campanelli, P. C., & Kloska, D. D. (1992). An elementary school-based alcohol misuse prevention program: A follow-up evaluation. *Journal of Studies on Alcohol, 53,* 106-121.

Smith, G. T., & Goldman, M. S. (1994). Alcohol expectancy theory and the identification of high-risk adolescents. *Journal of Research on Adolescence, 4,* 229-247.

Smith, G. T., Goldman, M. S., Greenbaum, P. E., & Christiansen, B. A. (1995). Expectancy for social facilitation from drinking: The divergent paths of high-expectancy and low-expectancy adolescents. *Journal of Abnormal Psychology, 10,* 32-40.

Smith, G. T., McCarthy, D. M., & Goldman, M. S. (1995). Self-reported drinking and alcohol-related problems among early adolescents: Dimensionality and validity over 24 months. *Journal of Studies on Alcohol, 56,* 383-394.

Spoth, R., & Redmond, C. (1996). Illustrating a framework for rural prevention research: Project Family studies of rural family participation and outcomes. In R. D. Peters & R. J. McMahon (Eds.), *Preventing childhood disorders, substance abuse, and delinquency* (pp. 299-328). Thousand Oaks, CA: Sage.

Spoth, R., Redmond, C., & Lepper, H. (in press). Alcohol initiation outcomes of universal family-focused preventive interventions: One-and two year follow-ups of a controlled study. *Journal of Studies on Alcohol.*

Spoth, R., Redmond, C., Hockaday, C., & Yoo, S. (1996). Protective factors and young adolescent tendency to abstain from alcohol use: A model using two waves of intervention study data. *American Journal of Community Psychology, 24,* 749-770.

Spoth, R., Redmond, C., & Shin, C. (1998). Direct and indirect latent-variable parenting outcomes of two universal family-focused preventive interventions: Extending a public health-oriented research base. *Journal of Consulting and Clinical Psychology, 66,* 385-399.

Stacy, A. W., Newcomb, M. D., & Bentler, P. M. (1992). Interactive and higher-order effects of social influences on drug use. *Journal of Health and Social Behavior, 33,* 226-241.

Stouthamer-Loeber, M., Loeber, R., Farrington, D. P., Zhang, Q., Van Kammen, W., & Maguin, E. (1993). The double edge of protective and risk factors for delinquency: Interrelations and developmental patterns. *Development and Psychopathology, 5,* 683-701.

Sussman, S., Petosa, R., & Clarke, P. (1996). The use of empirical curriculum development to improve prevention research. *American Behavioral Scientist, 39,* 838-852.

Swaim, R. C., Beauvais, F., Chavez, E. L., & Oetting, E. R. (1997). The effect of school dropout rates on estimates of adolescent substance use among three racial/ethnic groups. *American Journal of Public Health, 87,* 51-55.

Tarter, R. E. (1988). Are there inherited behavioral traits that predispose to substance abuse? *Journal of Consulting and Clinical Psychology, 56,* 189-196.

Tarter, R.E. (1990). Evaluation and treatment of adolescent substance abuse: A decision tree method. *American Journal of Drug and Alcohol Abuse, 16,* 1-46.

Tarter, R. E., & Hegedus, A. (1991). The Drug Use Screening Inventory: Its application in the evaluation and treatment of alcohol and drug abuse. *Alcohol Health and Research World, 15,* 65-75.

Thomasson, H. R., Crabb, D. W., & Edenberg, H. J. (1993). Alcohol and aldehyde dehydrogenase polymorphisms and alcoholism. *Behavior Genetics, 23,* 131-136.

Thompson, E. A., Horn, M., Herting, J. R., & Eggert, L. L. (1997). Enhancing outcomes in an indicated drug prevention program for high-risk youth. *Journal of Drug Education, 27,* 19-41.

Thompson, K. M., & Wilsnack, R. W. (1987). Parental influence on adolescent drinking: Modeling, attitudes, or conflict? *Youth and Society, 19,* 22-43.

Tubman, J. G., & Windle, M. (1995). Continuity of difficult temperament in adolescence: Relations with depression, life events, family support, and substance use across a one year period. *Journal of Youth and Adolescence, 24,* 133-153.

Tubman, J. G., Windle, M., & Windle, R. C. (1996). The onset and cross-temporal patterning of sexual intercourse in middle adolescence: Prospective relations with behavioral and emotional problems. *Child Development, 67,* 327-343.

University of Michigan News and Information Services. (1997, December 18). *Drug use among American teens shows some signs of leveling after a long rise* [Press release]. Ann Arbor: University of Michigan.

U.S. Department of Health and Human Services, Substance Abuse and Mental Health Services Administration. (1993). *National Drugs and Alcoholism Treatment Unit Survey (NDATUS): 1991 main report* (DHHS Pub. No. SMA 93-2007). Rockville, MD: Author.

Vaillant, G. E. (1983). *The natural history of alcoholism.* Cambridge, MA: Harvard University Press.

von Knorring, L., Palm, U., & Anderson, H. E. (1985). Relationship between treatment outcome and subtype of alcoholism in men. *Journal of Studies on Alcohol, 46,* 388-391.

Wagenaar, A. C. (1993). Minimum drinking age and alcohol availability to youth: Issues and research needs. In M. E. Hilton & G. Bloss (Eds.), *Economics and the prevention of alcohol-related problems* (pp. 175-200). Rockville, MD: National Institute on Alcoholism and Alcohol Abuse.

Wagenaar, A. C., Komro, K. A., McGovern, P., Williams, C. L., & Perry, C. L. (1993). Effects of a saliva test pipeline procedure on adolescent self- reported alcohol use. *Addiction, 88,* 199-208.

Wagenaar, A. C., & Wolfson, M. (1994). Enforcement of the legal minimum drinking age in the United States. *Journal of Public Health Policy, 15,* 37-53.

Wagenaar, A. C., & Wolfson, M. (1995). Deterring sales and provision of alcohol to minors: A study of enforcement in 295 counties in four states. *Public Health Reports,110,* 41-427.

Webb, J. A., & Baer, P. E. (1995). Influence of family disharmony and parental alcohol use on adolescent social skills, self-efficacy, and alcohol use. *Addictive Behaviors, 20*(1), 127-135.

Webb, J. A., Baer, P. E., McLaughlin, R. J., McKelvey, R. S., & Caid, C. D. (1991). Risk factors and their relation to initiation of alcohol use among early adolescents. *Journal of the American Academy of Child and Adolescent Psychiatry, 30,* 563-568.

Werch, C. E., & DiClemente, C. C. (1994). A multi-component stage model for matching drug prevention strategies and messages to youth stage of use. *Health Education Research, 9,* 37-46.

Werner, E. E., & Smith, R. S. (1982). *Vulnerable but invincible: A longitudinal study of resilient children and youth.* New York: McGraw-Hill.

Weschler, H., Davenport, A., Dowdall, G., Moeykens, B., & Castillo, S. (1994). Health and behavioral consequences of binge drinking in college: A national survey of students at 140 campuses. *Journal of the American Medical Association, 272,* 1672-1677.

West, S. G., & Aiken, L. S. (1997). Toward understanding individual effects in multicomponent prevention programs: Design and analysis strategies. In K. J. Bryant, M. Windle, & S. G. West (Eds.), *The science of prevention: Methodological advances from alcohol and substance abuse research* (pp. 167-209). Washington, DC: American Psychological Association.

Wheeler, K., & Malmquist, J. (1987). Treatment approaches in adolescent chemical dependency. *Pediatric Clinics of North America, 34,* 437-447.

White, H. R., & Huselid, R. F. (1997). Gender differences in alcohol use during adolescence. In R. W. Wilsnack & S. C. Wilsnack (Eds.), *Gender and alcohol: Individual and social perspectives* (pp. 176-198). New Brunswick, NJ: Rutgers Center of Alcohol Studies.

White, H. R., & Labouvie, E. W. (1989). Towards the assessment of adolescent problem drinking. *Journal of Studies on Alcohol, 50,* 30-37.

Williams, C. L., Perry, C. L., Farbakhsh, K., & Veblen-Mortenson, S. (in press). Project Northland: Comprehensive alcohol use prevention for young adolescents, their parents, schools, peers, and communities. *Journal of Studies on Alcohol.*

Wills, T. A., Windle, M., & Cleary, S. D. (1998). Temperament and novelty-seeking in adolescence: A test for convergence of dimensions of temperament with constructs from Cloninger's theory. *Journal of Personality & Social Psychology, 74,* 387-406.

Windle, M. (1991). Alcohol use and abuse: Some findings from the National Adolescent Student Health Survey. *Alcohol Health and Research World, 15,* 5-10.

Windle, M. (1994). A study of friendship characteristics and problem behaviors among middle adolescents. *Child Development, 65,* 1764-1777.

Windle, M. (1996). An alcohol involvement topology for adolescents: Convergent validity and longitudinal stability. *Journal of Studies on Alcohol, 57,* 627-637.

Windle, M. (in press). Critical conceptual measurement issues in the study of resilience. In M. S. Glantz, J. Johnson, & L. Huffman, (Eds.), *Resiliency and development: Positive life adaptations.* New York: Plenum.

Windle, M., & Barnes, G. M. (1988). Similarities and differences in correlates of alcohol consumption and problem behaviors among male and female adolescents. *International Journal of the Addictions, 23,* 707-728.

Windle, M., Barnes, G. M., & Welte, J. (1989). Causal models of adolescent substance use: An examination of gender differences using distribution-free estimators. *Journal of Personality and Social Psychology, 56,* 132-142.

Windle, M., & Blane, H. T. (1989). Cognitive ability and drinking behavior in a national sample of young adults. *Alcoholism: Clinical and Experimental Research, 13,* 43-48.

Windle, M., & Davies, P. T. (in press). Developmental theory and research. In K. E. Leonard & H. T. Blane (Eds.), *Psychological theories of drinking and alcoholism.* New York: Guilford.

Windle, M., Miller-Tutzauer, C., & Domenico, D. (1992). Alcohol use, suicidal behavior, and risky activities among adolescents. *Journal of Research on Adolescence, 2,* 317-330.

Windle, M., & Searles, J. S.(Eds.). (1990). *Children of alcoholics: Critical perspectives.* New York: Guilford.

Windle, M., & Tubman, J. G. (in press). Children of alcoholics: A developmental psychopathological perspective. In W. K. Silverman & T. Ollendick (Eds.), *Developmental issues in the clinical treatment of children and adolescents.* Needham Heights, MA: Allyn & Bacon.

Windle, M., & Windle, R. C. (1996). Coping strategies, drinking motives, and stressful life events among adolescents: Associations with emotional and behavioral problems, and academic functioning. *Journal of Abnormal Psychology, 105,* 551-560.

Winters, K. C. (1990). The need for improved assessment of adolescent substance involvement. *Journal of Drug Issues, 20,* 487-502.

Winters, K. C. (1992). Development of an adolescent alcohol and other drug abuse screening scale: Personal Experience Screening Questionnaire. *Addictive Behaviors, 17,* 479-490.

Winters, K. C., & Henly, G. A. (1993). *The adolescent diagnostic interview schedule and user's manual.* Los Angeles: Western Psychological Services.

Winters, K. C., Latimer, W. W., & Stinchfield, R. (in press). Examining psychosocial correlates of drug involvement among drug clinic-referred youth. *Psychology of Addictive Behaviors.*

Wolfson, M., Wagenaar, A. C., & Hornseth, G. W. (1995). Law officers' view of enforcement of the minimum drinking age: A four-state study. *Public Health Reports, 110,* 428-438.

Yu, J., & Williford, W. R. (1992). The age of alcohol onset and alcohol, cigarette, and marijuana use patterns: An analysis of drug use progression of young adults in New York State. *The International Journal of the Addictions, 27,* 1313-1323.

Zucker, R. A., & Gomberg, E. S. L. (1986). Etiology of alcoholism reconsidered. *American Psychologist, 41,* 783-793.

Zucker, R. A., Fitzgerald, H. E., & Moses, H. D. (1995). Emergence of alcohol problems and the several alcoholisms: A developmental perspective on etiologic theory and life course trajectory. In D. Cicchetti & D. J. Cohen (Eds.), *Developmental psychopathology* (Vol. 2: Risk, disorder and adaptation; pp. 677-711). New York: John Wiley.

Zuckerman, M. (1994). *Behavioral expressions and biosocial bases of sensation seeking.* New York: Cambridge University Press.

AUTHOR INDEX

SUBJECT INDEX

ABOUT THE AUTHOR

Michael Windle is Professor of Psychology and Director of the Doctoral Studies Program in Developmental Psychology at the University of Alabama at Birmingham. He received his PhD from the College of Human Development and Family Studies at Pennsylvania State University. Prior to this current appointment, he was Senior Research Scientist at the New York State Research Institute on Addictions in Buffalo, New York. He recently received an NIH MERIT Award for his prospective study of risk factors and adolescent drinking. Currently, he is an Associate Editor of *Alcoholism: Clinical and Experimental Research*, and on the Editorial Boards of *Developmental Psychology*, *Journal of Studies on Alcohol*, and *Journal of Adolescent Research*. His prior books include *Children of Alcoholics: Critical Perspectives* and *The Science of Prevention: Methodological Advances from Alcohol and Substance Abuse Research*.